103

OUT OF THIS WORLD

OUT OF THIS WORLD

ACROSS THE HIMALAYAS
TO TIBET

by

LOWELL THOMAS, Jr.

THE TRAVEL BOOK CLUB
121 CHARING CROSS ROAD
LONDON, W.C.2

THIS EDITION 1952

This edition by arrangement with
Macdonald & Co. (Publishers) Ltd.

Made and printed in Great Britain by
Purnell and Sons, Ltd.
Paulton (Somerset) and London

To

His Holiness, the Dalai Lama,

and

The People of Tibet, who

" . . . are earnestly praying that God will grant
happiness and everlasting peace to all humanity."

ACKNOWLEDGMENTS

The author acknowledges with gratitude the permission of the following publishers to reproduce quotations from copyright material: Harper & Brothers, New York, for *My Journey to Lhasa*, by Madame David-Neel, 1926; the Clarendon Press, Oxford, for *Tibet : Past and Present*, by Sir Charles Bell, 1924.

ABOUT THIS BOOK

Out of This World is the story of the trek my father and I made to the Dalai Lama's throne at Lhasa. This journey came as a climax to my father's lifetime of adventure. For me, it was probably the greatest travel adventure I will ever have, unless, someday, it will be possible to journey by space ship to another planet.

Words cannot express my everlasting gratitude to Dad, without whom I never would have seen the Forbidden Land. He had the dream and, in his incredible way, was able to make it come true.

There have been few books by Westerners about Tibet; fewer still with illustrations, and none, so far as I know, with pictures in colour. I am particularly proud that so many of my photographs could be included in this volume. They make a major contribution to our story.

For both of us, I wish to express our deep gratitude to all who helped our Tibetan caravan on to the Himalayan highroad to Lhasa—Ambassador Loy Henderson, Consul General Charles H. Derry, J. Jefferson Jones—then First Secretary at the United States Embassy—and Bob Burnett of Pan American Airways. We also wish to express our gratitude to Sir Girja Shankar Bajpai and all of his associates in the Indian Ministry of External Affairs, who co-operated with Ambassador Henderson. Without the help of these splendid people, getting to Lhasa would still be only a dream.

Very much in order is a special salute to publisher Ed Anthony of *Collier's* magazine and his editorial associates,

11

ABOUT THIS BOOK

whose enthusiasm and co-operation were an important factor in bringing this story to light.

I would like, also, to extend a low bow to Miss Elsie Weil, one of America's leading authorities on Asia, whose contribution by way of research, organization and editing has been invaluable in the setting down of this account of our crossing of the Himalayas to the Land of the Lamas.

L. T., JR.
Pawling, N. Y.

CONTENTS

13

LIST OF ILLUSTRATIONS

I

INVITATION TO LHASA

"THE MIRACLE HAS HAPPENED. MEET ME IN CALCUTTA. WE ARE ON OUR WAY TO LHASA."

With this breath-taking wireless, my father greeted me in Teheran on July 14, 1949, upon my return from a week's expedition among the Bakhtiari tribesmen of Eastern Iran with United States Supreme Court Justice William O. Douglas.

No one with a taste for adventure could fail to be pleased at receiving such news. As for me, I was so cheered with the prospect of leaving the hot barren plains of Iran that I literally turned cart wheels for joy. The film and study of Iran that I was in the process of completing could wait forever, for all I cared. Here was an opportunity that in all time has come to only a handful of Westerners—an invitation to enter the most remote and secluded of countries and to visit its capital, Lhasa.

Forbidden Tibet! Westerners have called it that for centuries. The mysterious mountain kingdom beyond the towering Himalayas on the very roof of the world has long been the Number One Eldorado for explorers and travellers with a keen appetite for the unknown. But since visitors from the West first found their way to Central Asia, only a few have been able to penetrate that sealed and silent land. Even fewer have been permitted to visit its fabulous capital, the sacred city of Lhasa, home of the Dalai Lama, religious and temporal ruler of Tibet, and spiritual head of millions of Buddhists in northern Asia.

You can well imagine my surprise on receiving that amazing telegram from my father. Before I shoved off for Persia we had talked briefly about the prospect of visiting Tibet. My father said that he intended to write to some friends in India about it. But the idea had struck me as so fantastic that I completely dismissed it from my mind.

What was the background of our incredible adventure? I must confess that I played no part in obtaining entrance permission from the Dalai Lama's government. That was entirely my father's doing.

It may be hackneyed to say so, but this trip seemed to be one of those dreams that come true. Perhaps Dad even had visions of Tibet when he was a boy in the old Colorado gold camp of Cripple Creek. At any rate, from the gold seekers he early acquired a determination to visit far-off places. And the desire to travel eventually nourished a craving to reach Tibet and make that almost impossible journey to Lhasa, because for centuries it has been the classic of the difficult.

As a young adventurer during and after World War I, my father was intrigued by three so-called forbidden spots on the globe—Arabia, Afghanistan and Tibet. Reaching Arabia first, Dad discovered a bonanza of romance in the person of Lawrence of Arabia, the fabulous young Englishman who led the Arab revolt in the war of the desert. That gave him a story to tell both in a book and on the lecture platform. Next he succeeded in getting into Afghanistan, realizing a second ambition. To the east of Afghanistan, beyond the lofty ranges of the Karakorams and Himalayas, lies Tibet, the goal of goals. Thirty years ago Dad arrived in India for two years of travel in Southern and Central Asia. At that time he had hopes of getting to Lhasa. But not a chance.

Other travels followed—a 28,000-mile flight to Europe, Asia and Africa in the primitive planes of 1926. On that trip he became acquainted with the jovial sailor Count

Felix von Luckner, who during World War I commanded a windjammer, sailing the Atlantic and Pacific as a daring sea raider. Luckner came to America with my father, who recorded his story in two books about the Sea Devil. But again he was recounting another's travels and adventures instead of his own.

Then came radio and long years of broadcasting the world's news; also days and nights of newsreel deadlines. During World War II there were hurried broadcasting journeys to other lands, including one around the world. On the latter Dad once more found himself deep in China along the Tibetan frontier.

Fortunately, I share my father's desire for travel and adventure. As a youngster, I made a voyage around Cape Horn with a United States Navy squadron. Later I joined a mountain-climbing expedition in Alaska. And after serving as an Air Force pilot during the last war, I flew to Bikini and on around the globe with Air Secretary W. Stuart Symington, now chairman of the National Security Resources Board. Then followed an expedition to Turkey, and another to Iran.

Although Dad had about given up hope of ever seeing Lhasa, he had not forgotten his old dream. So when, out of the blue, word came late in May, 1949, that he could get away for eight or ten weeks—his first real vacation in nineteen years on the air—it took him all of a minute to decide where he would like to go!

"Lhasa!" he confided to Mother. "Maybe it is impossible, especially on such short notice. Yet this is likely to be my one and only chance. A million-to-one shot, but I'll try."

Off went an air mail letter to Loy W. Henderson, Washington's new Ambassador to India. Congratulating him on his appointment, Dad added this postscript: "Now that you are in Hindustan, a land of miracles, how about performing a miracle? How about arranging for me, my son and three other Americans to visit Tibet? Is there any hope?"

The Ambassador promptly replied, explaining that the doors to Tibet seemed more tightly closed than ever. He also reminded my father that we have no official diplomatic contact with the Dalai Lama. Another friend in India, Sir Girja Shankar Bajpai, top official in Prime Minister Nehru's Ministry of External Affairs, confirmed what Loy Henderson had said. But apparently both Sir Girja and the Ambassador liked the idea, hopeless though it seemed, and sent my father's request across the Himalayas to Lhasa.

Miracles still happen! A midnight call came from our State Department, relaying a radio message from Tibet, via India, saying: "You are invited to Lhasa. Come at once." But permission was not granted for a party of five, only for Dad and me. We were to enter by way of Gangtok, capital of the Himalayan state of Sikkim, via the caravan route over Nathu-La, a 14,800-foot pass.

By this time two precious weeks of vacation had already gone by, and Dad knew he could not possibly make the trip, with all the caravan travel from India to Lhasa and back, in the time that remained. Part of the journey would have to be on his sponsor's time. That difficulty suggested another idea to complete the project. Why couldn't Dad resume his programme from Tibet—culminating with broadcasts from Lhasa? This certainly was piling fantasy on fantasy, since Tibet has no radio facilities and very little electricity.

However, there was a way out. New recording devices were available, portable recorders which could be used for long-distance broadcasts, even from the heart of Asia. Why not take those battery-driven outfits to Tibet? The sponsor was enthusiastic and gave my father a leave of absence to undertake a sort of broadcast-travel diary from the Roof of the World. While a number of big-name guest speakers would take his place on the show, Dad and I would come in from along the route, wherever possible, with our tape recorders.

As I set down our experiences here at home, I find it hard to believe that we ever were in Tibet. But a pair of crutches in the attic serves as a reminder of Dad's serious accident on the return trip from Lhasa to India and of those weeks the Tibetan villagers lifted and bounced and hoisted his litter over their mountain passes. Even so, it already seems that it must have happened to two other people. When we returned from this highest and most inaccessible of countries, we felt that we were coming out of the Seventh Century into the Twentieth. We were emerging from a land where there was little to remind us of the outside world. Once we crossed the Himalayas into Tibet we were indeed travellers in the land of the Lost Horizon. And it often seemed as though we were dreaming —acting the parts of characters in James Hilton's novel, on our way to Shangri-La.

Practically all grade-school pupils are familiar with that large area on the map of Central Asia marked with the word "Tibet." But until we went there, we had no conception of how remote it really is. The Antarctic region is usually considered the most distant spot on our planet. Still, it takes longer to get from any one of Tibet's neighbours to the capital city of Lhasa than to journey by sea from South America to the Antarctic.

By air? That's impossible, since the Tibetans absolutely forbid travel by air, by car, or even by carriage or cart. As far as transportation is concerned, Tibet is a country without a wheel. This seems incredible, considering that theirs is a civilization much older than our own. You can reach Lhasa only by making a long overland journey—a trip by caravan that takes from three to four months by many of the routes. And by the shortest route, with horses, yaks, mules and donkeys, a caravan will take from three to four weeks—assuming it carries the Dalai Lama's passport, guaranteeing assistance and safe passage.

Tibet's close neighbours are also difficult to reach. To the west is Ladakh, an outer province of Kashmir, sometimes called "Little Tibet." To the south are a group of partially explored semi-independent states: Nepal, which few Westerners have been allowed to enter; a wild, mountainous bit of Bengal; the picturesque mountain state of Sikkim, which is the main gateway to Tibet; the hermit country of Bhutan; and half-explored Himalayan sections of Assam and Burma. To the east of Tibet lies a part of China's Far West with which few Chinese are well acquainted—mountains inhabited by aboriginal tribes. Only a few Western missionaries, explorers and airmen have ever been there. To the north are those two vast, sparsely populated regions of lofty mountains and forbidding deserts—Russian and Chinese Turkistan, the latter now known as Sinkiang.

As for Tibet itself, nature has, for the most part, lavishly co-operated to isolate the people from undesired visitors—at least up to the present time. Far above the timberline, at altitudes averaging from 14,000 to 18,000 feet above sea level, this vast, wind-swept tableland is guarded by bleak deserts and a great girdle of glacier-crowned mountains, some five miles high. Two world wars have brought startling changes to most of the globe, but so far not to Tibet. It remains a feudal theocracy, ruled with an iron hand by two hundred thousand all-powerful Buddhist monks who have fiercely resisted nearly every attempt by unwelcome intruders to invade their solitude.

It is not surprising, therefore, that except for a few explorers, travellers and specialists, most Westerners are vaguely and often incorrectly informed about this mountain country in the heart of Central Asia, isolated both by geography and the will of its people.

For example, a popular and up-to-date American atlas

offers the following data on Tibet: "Nominally Chinese."
That's wrong. "Area—approximately 470,000 square
miles." Wrong. "Population—one million." That, too,
is wrong.

"What's the population of that little country?" a former
American editor and publisher asked us on our return
home.

"No census has ever been taken," we replied, "but most
estimates are between three and five million. And it isn't
such a little country—it's about one-third as large as the
United States, although the frontiers have been defined
only roughly."

Another query has frequently cropped up since our
return. Many persons have come to me after my illustrated
talk on Tibet with the comment: "A newsreel not long
ago showed India's Prime Minister Nehru landing at an
airfield in Tibet, and being greeted by the Dalai Lama.
So, when that accident happened to your father, why didn't
a rescue plane fly in and pick you both up? Why did he
have to be carried for sixteen days on the shoulders of
Tibetans?" Well, the newsreel must have photographed
two other persons in a different country. First of all,
Prime Minister Nehru has never been in Tibet. Second,
no aeroplane is allowed to land there. Of course, a plane
might accidentally crash in Tibet. This actually happened
to five American Air Force men during World War II.

We had a long discussion with a Tibetan official in
Gyantse, trying to determine why these people are so
insistent on shutting out the rest of the world.

"Don't you want *any* of the conveniences of the modern
age?" we asked.

"Well—perhaps." He hesitated. "We are willing to
accept them as we accept alms."

The lamas invariably give the same answer. They are
convinced that they alone of all peoples are not slaves to
the gadgets and whirring wheels of the industrial age.

They want no part of it. To them the devices, doodads and super-yoyos—the symbols of our Western civilization —are toys, of no real value. To them—or so they want you to believe—only the things of the mind are of lasting importance.

So that's why, in a land about one-third the size of the United States, with a population of about four million, you find no aeroplanes, motor cars, railways, wagons, bicycles, factories, hospitals, newspapers, magazines, plumbing, running water, heating and sewerage systems—in fact almost none of the mechanical devices and services that we regard as necessities of life. It should be mentioned that a few of the lay-nobles and traders who send caravans to India and China have battery-operated radios. Also, one generator in Lhasa supplies electricity to the dim bulbs in a few buildings. Although Tibet turns a cold shoulder on modern conveniences, it must not be inferred that it is a primitive, uncultured nation. On the contrary, without benefit of science, the land of the Dalai Lama has maintained a unique and individual civilization of high order for many centuries, especially in art, architecture, religious philosophy, literature and folklore.

A British authority on Tibet, Graham Sandberg, in *The Exploration of Tibet*, wrote in 1904: "Those, who from the outer world have gained entrance to Tibet and made real journeys in the country, still form a select and notable body of men." And that statement *still* stands. The Tibetans, inherently suspicious of all foreigners, want it that way.

Is it any wonder then that so few Westerners have gazed upon the radiance and splendour of the cluster of golden roofs which is the traveller's first view of Lhasa as he rounds the last mountain?

In the seventeenth and eighteenth centuries a few European missionaries trickled into Tibet, but they did not succeed in establishing a permanent foothold. A handful of other Europeans followed later—many of them distinguished explorers and geographers, who faced untold perils and travelled in disguise. From 1904, when Britain sent a military expedition to Tibet to gain trade concessions, until India won her independence in 1947, British trade and political agents kept in close touch with Tibet, but mostly from the Indian side of the border.

As for Americans, many have tried but only a few have reached Lhasa. In fact we were the seventh and eighth to be permitted to visit Lhasa, and the fourth and fifth to be received officially by the Tibetan ruler, who is worshipped as a god. Suydam Cutting, naturalist and leader of museum expeditions, was the first of our countrymen to reach Lhasa. That was in 1935. Two years later he was invited to return with his wife. The Cuttings surely would have met the Dalai Lama had not the throne been unoccupied from 1933 to 1940. The third American to enter the Holy City was Theos Bernard of Arizona. In 1942, two United States Army officers, Lieutenant Colonel Ilia Tolstoy and Captain Brooke Dolan, became the first and second Americans to have an audience with the Dalai Lama. They were sent by the Office of Strategic Services to find, if they could, some new Central Asian route to ship supplies to besieged China. The sixth on the Lhasa scene, and the third to meet His Holiness, also during World War II, was Arch Steele, then a Chicago *Daily News* foreign correspondent, who wrote an informative series on Lamaland. We were to be next.

2

PREPARATIONS FOR THE JOURNEY

AFTER Dad's message about Tibet, I left Teheran in double-quick time for Basra, at the head of the Persian Gulf. From that busy Iraqi seaport, celebrated as the home of Sinbad the Sailor and today the principal shipping centre for the world's dates, I took off comfortably for India on one of Pan American's flying carpets.

My clipper set me down in Calcutta several days ahead of my father. That barely gave me time to round up the equipment and supplies needed for our expedition. I had arrived at the height of the monsoon season, when the skies open up at any inconvenient hour of day or night. The streets were like rivers, and Calcutta's teeming millions waded through them with their shoes under their arms, while I splashed from shop to shop picking up supplies.

Fortunately, most of the preliminary groundwork for the expedition had been taken care of. Our consul general in Calcutta, Charles Derry, had considerately surveyed a number of shops to determine where I could find what would best suit our needs. Jefferson Jones, first secretary of our embassy in Delhi, who had come down to Calcutta to give Mr. Derry a hand, had arranged about passes for the border province of Sikkim, as well as for the *lamyik*, our Tibetan visa, without which no Westerner can travel safely in Tibet.

To set out on a trek like this over the highest mountain ranges and into the most remote country in the world means very careful planning. If I forgot something essential, it would be just our bad luck. No hotels or lunch wagons along this trail! To mention only a few items, our equipment included saddles and bridles, army cots, and sleeping bags, mosquito netting, flashlights, a portable table, two portable chairs, a canvas bath (which we never used!), and tarpaulins to keep our packs dry while moving up through the rainy forest of Sikkim to the Tibetan plateau. Our clothing on the trail would be warm ski pants, ski boots, woollen shirts, sweaters, windbreakers, ski caps, and rubberized rain suits—all flown out with Dad.

A first-rate medical kit is a must on an extended journey into remote country where there is no modern medicine— and Tibet has next to none. But, in my frantic hurry, I failed to give this matter adequate attention. The kit I threw together was designed to take care of such problems as leech bites, minor cuts, malaria, dysentery, and head-aches; and it fell far short of our needs when we ran into heavy going on the return from Lhasa, for it contained no sedatives or splints. (See the Appendix for an ideal list of equipment.)

In Calcutta I also rounded up a complete kitchen, every-thing from pots and pans to dish towels. The most impor-tant kitchen item, next to the cook, of course, whom we acquired later, was the portable primus cooker of American make, which I had with me in Iran. A handy gadget on any expedition, the Colman primus heated things quickly for us with its blowtorch flame. Without it some of our food would have been served practically raw. We used our stove even in Tibetan kitchens, whenever we could, since we did not particularly relish the peculiar and penetrating flavour of food prepared over a yak-dung fire.

We expected to live off the land to some extent, but to be on the safe side I bought enough food to keep us going for more than a month. At the Great Eastern grocery I made up eight cases of food, each case weighing sixty-five pounds, each containing enough food to last both of us for six days.

Breakfast on the road to Lhasa would consist of stewed prunes or apple rings, followed by a large bowl of oatmeal or cream of wheat, canned bacon, crackers, jam and butter. As for liquids, we could have our choice of Ovaltine, coffee, tea or cocoa, topped off with powdered milk and sugar. Lunch, which we expected to eat in the saddle, would be simple but concentrated: crackers and cheese, sardines, chocolate, dried raisins, dates and figs. Our big meal was to come in the evening at the end of a long, fatiguing day of hiking and riding. After a bowl of bouillon we would have more buttered crackers and jam, then a plate of hot canned roast beef, veal or salmon, together with any fresh vegetables that we could buy along our way. Dessert would usually be dried fruit again, since Tibet is too cold to grow fruit, except for some peaches and apricots in the warmer, low-lying eastern valleys. Then more tea, cocoa or Ovaltine.

What our food lacked in variety was compensated by concentrated energy, most essential in the rugged marches over high mountain trails.

Before heading out across the Pacific by plane to join me in Calcutta, my father got in touch with Suydam Cutting, the naturalist and explorer, mentioned earlier as the first American to receive an official invitation to Lhasa. With not one, but three journeys into Tibet to his credit, he knew all the ropes. His suggestions were invaluable. He listed essential supplies and told Dad how short-cuts could be taken in the brief time we had to get ready. Every day on the trail we were grateful for his hint to pack our food in special cases—each one a complete unit containing everything needed from soup to salt—thus eliminating a frantic hunt through all the boxes at every stop.

Suydam Cutting's instructions on what to do and what not to do saved us from making too many awkward blunders in our contact with a people who for centuries have had their own sharply defined rules of courtesy and politeness, very different from our own. For example, he warned us to carry gifts for the Dalai Lama and high dignitaries in Lhasa, as well as for other officials along the way. Not only are gifts elaborately exchanged in Tibet. We had to be provided with a bale of visiting cards. When you pay a call on a Tibetan, you present a white silk scarf, a *kata*. The host, in turn, presents his *kata*. The exchange is quite an elaborate and punctilious ceremony.

Many journeys to Asia on natural history expeditions had taken Suydam Cutting to the fringes of Tibet. Naturally his appetite was whetted to cross the border and reach Lhasa, but he would not attempt the trip without official permission. On his first visit in 1930, he went as far as Gyantse, not too hard to negotiate, since the British were then issuing a few permits to that trading point, in accordance with a special treaty they had with Tibet. Home again, he never lost sight of his objective. To the thirteenth Dalai Lama, predecessor of the youth who is now temporal and religious head of Tibet, Cutting sent presents—among them such gifts as books on American architecture, a self-winding gold wrist watch, a glass cocktail shaker with a churn, which could be used to mix His Holiness's buttered tea, a pair of Dalmatian and of German hounds. His Holiness in turn sent Cutting a pair of Apsos, a special breed of Tibetan dog, with the plea to "take great care of them." All this resulted in a remarkable and unparalleled correspondence between a private American citizen and the supreme ruler of Tibet, worshipped as a living god. Sometimes the thirteenth Dalai Lama even asked Cutting to go to Washington on missions that might lead to more direct relations between Tibet and the United States.

Considering all the cordial and flourishing communications with the Dalai Lama, Cutting hoped he would soon receive an invitation to Lhasa. But none was forthcoming. Finally, on Christmas Day, 1933, he had a cable from the Kashag, the Supreme Council of Tibet, with news of the "temporary passing away of His Holiness" on December 17.

Suydam Cutting now wondered if he ever would see Lhasa. But, persevering, he transferred his friendly attentions to the Kashag and the Regent. Finally, in 1935, he received his long-hoped-for permission. Once in Lhasa, he made such a favourable impression on the authorities, partly because he himself thoroughly liked and admired the Tibetans, that he was invited to return in 1937 and bring his wife. He says in his book, *The Fire Ox and Other Years*, "It was the first time an invitation had ever been extended to a white woman for an unlimited stay."

The Cuttings were warmly received in Lhasa. The government placed at their disposal a charming house—Zara Linga—set in a private park, with willow groves and a little stream winding through the green lawns. During their occupancy, a group of young lamas from the Potala had a ten-day outing in the private park—a good opportunity to observe future Tibetan leaders enjoying their games, relaxation and outdoor feasting. In turn, the lamas, equally curious about the strangers, especially Mrs. Cutting, came in droves to the house.

When the Cuttings were in Lhasa the search was still being made for the child who would be the reincarnation of the thirteenth Dalai Lama. They had many visits and conversations with the Regent and high officials. They were banqueted and entertained at elaborate parties and outdoor fêtes by the four hundred of Lhasa society, and overwhelmed with presents—everything from food to Tibetan rugs. When the Cuttings took to the trail again, heading for the high passes and India, they left many friends behind them in Lhasa—young and old.

We certainly found ourselves at an advantage, owing to Suydam Cutting's knowledge of Tibetan travel and

Tibetan customs. But with all the extremely practical advice he gave, he did make one suggestion that didn't work out as he had expected. When he made his treks to the Roof of the World, the Tibetans were more interested in hard currency than in paper money. With the British Raj still ruling India, the Tibetans favoured Indian rupees. Cutting had carried burlap bags of the heavy stuff across the mountains and he urged us to do the same. So we converted about $1,000 into stacks and stacks of rupees, half rupees, two-anna and one-anna coins.

Uniformed chaprassis at the bank carried those six burlap bags of Indian money out to the United States Consulate car. Escorted by Consul General Derry, we took the bags to his home. Then, under guard, to the swarming railway station. We slept with the money on the train. At Gangtok, in Sikkim, we had three strong wooden cases made. Each, with its bags of coin, weighed around sixty pounds. On the trail we slept with the boxes between our beds. And by day, as we rode along canyon walls, we were constantly apprehensive that our rupees would wind up at the bottom of a river. During our twenty-four days on the trail, it took one and a half mules, or yaks, just to carry our hard cash, always under close guard.

With much trouble and worry we lifted those boxes over the Himalayas to Lhasa—with their two hundred pounds of coins. But, at the Dalai Lama's capital, we were told that the Tibetans no longer wanted the stuff. Now they preferred paper money—either Indian or their own! And each time we flashed our coins they would demand a much more generous exchange rate or would flatly refuse to touch them. It would have been far better to have taken a roll of bills in a hip-pocket. We were about resigned to packing those two hundred pounds of money back to India when, at the last minute, an ex-top official, the Tibetan Croesus, Tsarong Shapé, heard of our predicament and took the bags of coins off our hands.

3

WHY WE WERE INVITED

W HY had we been so lucky? How had we come to be invited to the Land of the Lamas? What had caused the young Dalai Lama and his advisers to comply so promptly with our request to visit Lhasa? Countless pleas for admission are sent from every corner of the globe, but they are ignored.

As my father and I rounded narrow ledges along the steep canyon walls and slowly mounted the dizzy mountain passes on the ancient caravan route to the Holy City, in August, 1949, we talked over these questions. No explanation had been given to us. All we knew was that, happily for us, permission had come through without delay. We suspected that the answer was one word: Communism. The Tibetan officials in Lhasa later confirmed our hunch.

Tibet fears Communism. By the summer of 1949 the Chinese Reds had brought most of China under their control and made it clear that when the China job was finished Tibet would be their next objective. This was the chief topic of conversation when we reached Lhasa. Acutely aware of the Reds' intentions, the Lhasa government was considering how America might be made to realize Tibet's serious problem of defence against Asiatic Communism. Moreover, they wanted America and all the world to know that they are now, and have always considered themselves, an independent nation.

At the psychological moment, when the top Tibetan officials were debating what would be the best way to inform America of the Red threat to Tibet, our request was forwarded from India. They decided to take a gamble —and we were invited to Lhasa. So ours was the once-in-three-lifetimes opportunity to travel into the heart of an incredible, fabulous, story-book country—a journey taking us "out of this world."

Why should this small country, whose people only want to be left alone to mind their own affairs and live in their unique culture undisturbed, why should it be threatened? And why should we, on the other side of the world, be concerned?

The peril is imminent. On the north and east are innumerable victorious Chinese Communist troops who have been practically idle following the rapid collapse of the Nationalist government. The Communist radio in China has broadcast a number of times within recent months its plans to "liberate" Tibet. The Tibetans may lack modern conveniences, but their government heads are intelligent and fully aware of the havoc and misery Communist "liberation" has wrought in other small countries. At the time of our visit only ten thousand Tibetan troops, armed with obsolete weapons, stood behind the mountain barrier to safeguard their homeland. We were told that another hundred thousand were being hurriedly mobilized and armed with light weapons purchased from India, but without the most up-to-date equipment and training they might not be enough protection against fanatical Communist hordes.

The Communists covet Tibet for several reasons. If they gain control of the Holy City of Lhasa, they can wield tremendous influence over the Central and Eastern Asian Buddhist world. But the main reason is strategic, for possession of Tibet would give them an 1,800-mile frontier with India and an ideal jumping-off spot, mostly downhill, for an army to invade the vast peninsula of Hindustan and dominate its four hundred million people.

Tibet is all that stands between the Red armies of China and India. And India holds the key to the domination of the whole continent of Asia.

Then there is the significance of Tibet's mineral wealth. About a year ago the British Foreign Office announced that expeditions in Tibet had discovered "mineral deposits of unascertainable value." The London dispatch implied that this new find was radio-active metal—the material of the atomic bomb. Further evidence that the high spot of the world is fast becoming a hot spot was produced with the reports that Soviet Russia is extending a chain of air bases down through Central Asia toward Tibet and that a modern military highway is being constructed by the Chinese Communists through their western provinces to the Tibetan border.

Recently we had an amazing indication of Moscow's zealous interest in Tibet, when the Soviet weekly, *New Times*, official organ of the Kremlin, attacked us editorially. The publication charged we had been sent to Tibet by the United States Government to try to tear that country away from China and turn it into an Anglo-American colony! The *New Times* said that my father and I had been "given a very important role by the United States Government" for what the Russian journal labelled "a dirty adventure." (Dirty is a favourite Soviet adjective.)

Here's the latest Kremlin twister, broadcast by the Czechoslovak Red radio and designed to pave the way for invasion: "The strategic position of Tibet and its uranium ore stimulated the Washington strategists to gain influence over Tibet. A year ago," says the Communist propaganda, "an American expedition was sent to Tibet, headed by an agent of the O.S.S.—Lowell Thomas, who modestly calls himself a radio commentator." These are the words from Red Prague.

So, to the liars in the Kremlin, who falsify just about everything, my Dad is not a radio commentator, but a special government agent. There are no limits to what the Communists will say if they think what they say will help them gain their point. Surely a house built on such shifting sands—on a fabric of lies—will collapse! Not only had there been no consultation with officials in Washington previous to our journey, but in my father's haste to get off he failed to ask President Truman if he wanted to send a gift or letter to the Dalai Lama. This is a customary courtesy—a gesture that should never be neglected by anyone fortunate enough to be invited to the Forbidden City.

Then, as my father's radio listeners well know, the whole affair was about as private as a fish bowl. We sent frequent recordings back to America, describing our journey into and over the Himalayas and the interviews we had with prominent Tibetans. These recordings went out both by long and short wave over a vast radio network on Dad's nightly CBS news show. So there was nothing secret or confidential about any part of our journey.

Ours was decidedly *not* a government mission, but we had every intention of openly informing the American people of whatever we could learn about the growing crisis with which Tibet was confronted—and with Tibet, the nations of the free world.

Some of the most fruitful talks we had in Lhasa were with Tibet's two astute foreign ministers, a monk named Luishahr Dzaza Lama and Surkhang Dzaza, a layman—both recognized authorities on Tibetan history. Seated in their office in a building next to Lhasa's sacred Cathedral known as the Jokang, we were offered an illuminating perspective of Tibet's two main problems: Communism and China. We asked them about rumours we had heard in India that there had been a Communist revolt in Lhasa in which a number of Chinese and Tibetans had been killed.

"Not true!" both ministers exclaimed simultaneously in vigorous Tibetan, translated by our interpreter.

Their explanation of this rumour is significant, since Tibet abhors as well as fears Communism, which is contrary to its whole philosophy of life, and since Tibetans are not exactly enthusiastic that they have to accept the geographical fact that Red China is their next-door neighbour. But first I shall try to sum up briefly the background of Chinese-Tibetan relations, as the two ministers put it to us.

Historically, geographically and culturally there have been close ties between China and Tibet for many centuries. Evidence of this abounds today. Tibetans on the eastern plateau nearest the Chinese border have adopted many Chinese customs, from chopsticks to pigtails. The Chinese have given up the pigtails, but upper-class Tibetans still wear them. Wealthy Tibetans are robed in Chinese silks and embellish their homes with Chinese furniture and porcelain. Since before America was discovered, caravans have plodded wearily over the ancient and difficult trade routes, bringing Tibetan wool to China and Chinese brick tea to Tibet. The great Tibetan monasteries are filled with priceless old Chinese treasures, the gifts of Chinese emperors.

From the seventh to the ninth centuries of our era Tibet and China were constantly at war. The Tibetans had not yet fallen under the peaceful influence of Buddhism. Then they were one of the great military powers of Asia and could give as well as take the blows. In the middle of the seventh century the Chinese captured Lhasa but, in A.D. 766, Tibet won an overwhelming victory over the Chinese, who had to pay a large tribute to save their capital, at that time Chang-an. Again, a few years later, Tibet overran western China. This time the Chinese had to sign a treaty by which Lake Koko Nor was fixed as the north-eastern boundary of Tibet. Thus the Tibetans held fast to their beloved mountain country.

What the Tibetans lost in martial spirit with the rise of Buddhism, they gained in religious influence. Kublai

Khan, founder of the Mongol Dynasty of China, was converted to the lamaistic form of Buddhism by the high priest of Sakya monastery near Lhasa, and the great Khan, with one of his grand gestures, graciously appointed the monk secular ruler of Tibet. Thus began the reign of Tibetan priest-kings. In time Mongolia was completely converted to Tibetan Buddhism. It was the Mongols during the reign of Altan Khan, who first gave the monk-ruler at Lhasa the title: Dalai Lama Vajradhara, which means the All-embracing Lama, the Holder of the Thunderbolt. The spiritual supremacy and religious authority of the Dalai Lama were accepted in China, Mongolia and many Central Asian regions, as well as in his own country. When the fifth Dalai Lama—known as the Great Fifth—came to Peiping in the early years of the Manchu Dynasty, the Emperor met him a day's journey from the capital. At the Imperial Palace the Emperor stepped down from the Dragon Throne and advanced to greet him, indicating that the Dalai Lama was regarded as an independent ruler—a remarkable concession in the days when Chinese emperors had it pretty much their own way —at least in China.

It was, however, under the Manchus, from the seventeenth through the nineteenth century, that China tightened its control on Tibet. Chinese Residents, known as Ambans, were stationed permanently in Lhasa. Tibet sent annual tribute to Peiping. It was the Chinese, we were told, not the Tibetans, who spread abroad the impression that Tibet was a forbidden country. As long as the Chinese did not interfere too much in internal affairs, this arrangement suited the Tibetans perfectly, since they did not want encroachments by other countries. As a matter of fact, as the Manchu power grew weaker, their control over Tibet slackened. China, regarding Tibet as an "outer province," always had difficulty in administering its outer provinces. In the latter part of the nineteenth century, Tibet was practically free of any real Chinese domination, due to the efforts of the thirteenth Dalai Lama.

In 1911, when the Sun Yat-sen revolution forced out the Manchus to make way for the Chinese Republic, the Tibetans declared their freedom, formally ending China's suzerainty and packing the Ambans back to China.

"Ever since then Tibet has been completely independent," said Surkhang Dzaza, tapping his red lacquer table with a bamboo pen. And Luishahr, the red-robed monk, nodded enthusiastically in agreement.

But the Chinese never officially recognized Tibet's declaration of independence. When the thirteenth Dalai Lama died in 1933, Chiang Kai-shek's government sent a mission to Lhasa to express deep sympathy. Part of this mission, equipped with a wireless sending set, stayed on, allegedly to settle boundary disputes. Tibet considered the Chinese group temporary, but the Chinese regarded it as permanent. When the present Dalai Lama was enthroned in the capital in 1940, another mission arrived from China for the ceremony. Both the Chinese envoy and the British representative were admitted to the Potala for the enthronement ceremony. Later the Chinese press reported that the Chinese envoy, escorting the Dalai Lama to his throne, announced the installation. Then, according to the Chinese report, the little Dalai Lama prostrated himself in gratitude, implying submission. The Tibetans indignantly deny this, but unfortunately they have no news service to refute false statements or to present to the world their own version of what happens in Tibet. Most of the Chinese who came for the enthronement also stayed on in Lhasa, together with a detachment of Chinese troops.

In 1945 the Tibetans urged Chiang Kai-shek to admit Tibet's autonomy officially, but the Generalissimo kept putting them off. He had always insisted that as far as foreign affairs were concerned, Tibet was an outer province of China. The Tibetans strongly disclaimed his assertion, and they gave little heed to it. At that time it did not mean much to them, one way or the other. As a closed country, they had no problems in foreign affairs, only trade relations with India and China.

Then a real threat appeared on the horizon. Civil war broke out in China. The Chinese Reds were winning. The Nationalist Government was losing on all sides. The Dalai Lama's advisers, fearing that when the Reds controlled all of China they would also lay plans to absorb Tibet, took steps to oust the Chinese officials who had come with the special missions to Lhasa and stayed on as permanent but unwelcome residents. The Tibetan officials figured out that the new Red regime in China would want to send its own mission to Lhasa. And Chinese Communists in Tibet would increase the danger of Soviet Russia's infiltration into this most religious of Buddhist countries.

The Tibetan government decided to make its position clear without delay—to deny that Tibet had been even in the shadow of Chinese influence since 1911, when it announced its complete independence from China. Then, if the Nationalists were driven from China by the Reds, the Tibetans could say to Mao Tse-tung's Communist government: "We are an independent country, just as you are. We are not saying that you can't send a diplomatic envoy to Lhasa, but you can't tell us how to run our own affairs."

This was also the moment, the two ministers told us, to get rid of all those suspected of being Communist sympathizers. A Chinese restaurant in Lhasa, which had been spotted as an informal meeting place for agitators, was closed. The Chinese were invited to a garden party. It was all very friendly and very correct. They bowed low to one another. They drank tea together. Then the Tibetans, with urbane oriental courtesy, told the Chinese that they must leave at once.

The next day eighty to one hundred Chinese, with wives and children, were escorted on their way out of the country by a guard of honour headed by a general and a ranking lama. Presents of food and money were given to the Chinese. The most delightful and characteristically Tibetan touch was the band dispatched to play continuously for the entertainment of the departing "guests" on the difficult eighteen-day trip to Yatung, not far from the Indian frontier. This all happened about a month before our arrival.

"So you see," concluded Surkhang Dzaza, "far from being a Communist revolt, this incident, so twisted by outside rumours, was quite the opposite."

Tibet, we were given to understand, had used the expulsion of the Chinese to show the world in general and the Communists in particular that it was completely independent and would brook no outside interference—unless forced to submit to military conquest. That, alas, is the rub.

The thirteenth Dalai Lama was endowed with exceptional capacities, both as a secular and as a religious ruler. Two years before he died or, as the Tibetans say, departed to the "Heavenly Field," he wrote a long and remarkable letter to his people, who call it the Precious Protector's Last Testament. He seemed to have a prophetic vision of the troubles that were likely to visit his beloved country, high in the clouds. I should like to quote a passage from the translation made by Sir Charles Bell:

"The present is the time of the Five Kinds of Degeneration in all countries. In the worst class is the manner of working among the Red people. [The reference here is to the U.S.S.R.] They do not allow search to be made for the new Incarnation of the Grand Lama of Urga. They have seized and taken away all the sacred objects from the monasteries. They have made monks to work as soldiers. They have broken religion, so that not even the name of it remains. Have you heard of all these things that have happened at Urga? And they are still continuing.

WHY WE WERE INVITED

"It may happen that here in the centre of Tibet the Religion and the secular administration may be attacked both from the outside and from the inside. Unless we can guard our own country, it will now happen that the Dalai and Panchen Lamas, the Father and the Son, the Holders of the Faith, the glorious Rebirths, will be broken down and left without a name. As regards the monasteries and the priesthood, their land and other properties will be destroyed. The administrative customs of the Three Religious Kings will be weakened. The officers of the State, ecclesiastical and secular, will find their lands seized and their other property confiscated, and they themselves made to serve their enemies, or wander about the country as beggars do. All beings will be sunk in great hardship and in overpowering fear; the days and the nights will drag on slowly in suffering.

"Do not be traitors to Church and State by working for another country against your own. Tibet is happy, and in comfort now; the matter rests in your own hands. All civil and military matters should be organized with knowledge; act in harmony with each other; do not pretend that you can do what you cannot do. The improvement of the secular administration depends on your ecclesiastical and secular officials. High officials, low officials and peasants must all act in harmony to bring happiness to Tibet: one person alone cannot lift a heavy carpet; several must unite to do so."

The thirteenth Dalai Lama seemed to understand the Communist technique of boring from within as well as of invading from without. That they should work together in unity and harmony was the best advice he could offer his people as a weapon against a menace he recognized twenty years ago. He had no illusions that Tibet, alone and unaided, could put up a military defence against the rising tide of Communist aggression.

It is a year now since our visit to Lhasa. As I write,

newspaper reports of the Tibetan situation grow increasingly ominous. Some say that eight hundred thousand Chinese Communists are poised on the Sikang border ready to invade Tibet. Others claim that Red troops have already moved across the Tibetan frontier. None of the rumours has been definitely corroborated as yet. However, one thing is certain. The Tibetans, who had hoped for some support from the West or from India, have become discouraged. An eight-member Tibetan delegation headed by Tsipon Shakabpa, has gone to India for the purpose of making as favourable terms as possible with Peiping; independence if possible; if not, local autonomy. No one can predict tomorrow's move. The Land of the Lamas may be the next small country on the Communists' list for extinction.

4

OFF TO GANGTOK

WHEN an expedition bound for Tibet leaves Calcutta, it looks like Ringling, Barnum and Bailey emerging from winter quarters. But against an oriental background, it is even more colourful than the circus. An army of coolies handled our cases: food, clothing, presents, camping gear, film for six cameras, recording equipment and one iron trunk filled with those heavy bags of hard currency.

We left the last night of July for the railroad centre of Siliguri, at the foot of the mighty Himalayas, three hundred miles north of Calcutta. Squeezed into the train compartment with us were a ton of supplies and Johnny Roberts of Wakefield, Massachusetts, a young photographer, who had been working with me in Iran. We had special permission to take him on the first part of the journey, over the main chain of the Himalayas, to a point about four miles inside Tibet. We stacked our cases of food against the compartment doors and bolted the windows as a precaution against burglary. Passengers on that night train have frequently been robbed, some even murdered. None of us did much sleeping as we rattled north across the plains of Bengal.

Nearing Siliguri in the morning, we looked out the train window. Before us, rising above the green-jungled foothills of Sikkim and set in a cold blue sky, loomed the towering snow-capped peaks of the most formidable mountain wall in the world. Dominating the range, its summit far above its neighbours, was Kinchinjunga, third highest mountain on the earth, soaring 28,146 feet above sea level. That's almost twice as high as California's Mount Whitney, our loftiest peak. Kinchinjunga, rising like a lone sentinel in all its majesty from the flat Bengal plain, is even more impressive and awe-inspiring than Everest, loftiest of all mountains, located in the midst of other high peaks farther to the west on the Tibet-Nepal border. The mountain folk have a charming legend about Kinchinjunga. They say it is the home of a spirit who, in the form of a goose, showed the way over the mountain passes to the monk who brought the message of Buddhism to Sikkim.

At Siliguri we were met by a bus driver representing our transportation agent in Gangtok. He was called Lulu, and Lulu certainly lived up to his name! With the usual bickering and shouting over baksheesh a score of Bengali in turbans and G strings transferred our thirty-seven boxes and pieces of luggage to Lulu's truck for the seventy-mile trip to Gangtok, capital of Sikkim, where we were to organize our Tibetan caravan. Piling into Lulu's war-weary British lorry, we plunged into the jungle and snorted up a mountain road. A spectacular road it was—narrow, steep and winding. The jungle growth was thick around us and the muddy Tista, swollen with monsoon rains, flowed nearby. Once a big monkey excitedly crossed the road just ahead of Lulu's truck.

After several hours of slow climbing, during which we waited nervously for one of the bulging tyres to blow out, we came to a small village. Here we bought several delicious pineapples and bananas, our first good meal in twenty-four hours. A bit farther along we had to halt to show our passes at the Sikkim frontier. At the boundary line was a bridge to which were attached about one hundred white prayer flags, many in tatters, on which Buddhist prayers were inscribed. It is believed that each time the flags flutter in the breeze the prayers are transmitted to the Buddhist spiritual world.

At the twenty-mile point in our narrow road we were stopped by an old slide. It took more than two hours of hard labour to carry our baggage over the obstruction and transfer it to another dilapidated lorry. On we chugged, but before we had time to wipe the sweat from our brows the brakes screeched and brought us to another abrupt halt. Lulu and the two coolies began to jabber excitedly.

"It's a slip—a slip!" they cried, pointing to a billowing cloud of dust rising above the jungle half a mile ahead.

"How can it be?" I questioned. "Surely no landslide could raise such a cloud of dust."

But we soon found out! Up ahead the road was blocked by an immense wall of rock, dirt and stripped tree trunks, a huge tongue reaching out of the jungle on our right and spilling into the Tista River on the left. One look at the boiling cloud of pulverized rock showed that the slide must have come down just before we came along. The whole side of a mountain had collapsed under the monsoon rains. A mile and a half of jungle had slipped into the Tista, and the debris filled the road to a height of two hundred feet for a quarter of a mile. Natives who had been near the spot told us that the slide came down with a roar like thunder and that the swift-flowing river, powerful as its current was from the monsoon rains, was blocked off for several minutes until it built up enough pressure to sweep boulders and trees out of the way.

We had no chance of getting across or around the slide that day. Fortunately, nearby was one of the many shelters provided for stranded wayfarers in the mountain states on the Indian side of the Himalayas. So we thankfully took possession of the empty bungalow for the night.

Too stimulated by our first day on the road to turn in immediately after a makeshift supper, Johnny, Dad and I sat around for a while. We plunged into a discussion about that prince of travellers, Marco Polo. He covered more of Asia than any other traveller of the Middle Ages. When the famous Venetian crossed the Pamirs of Central Asia, he was not far from Tibet. But he never swerved from his caravan route on the way to the court of the great Kublai Khan to make a side trip south to the mysterious country, where, he said, the people performed the most "extraordinary marvels and sorceries by diabolic art." In his book he has a whole chapter on Tibet, not very flattering to Tibetans or their customs. Marco Polo must have collected his information second-hand from prejudiced Chinese. Just the same, some of Marco Polo's comments were true in his own thirteenth century and are still true today. Many travellers who have written of their Tibetan journeys have been only to its borders. And their books contain very little about the real Tibet. Comparatively few volumes in our western libraries have authentic information about this strange land. And so unchanged has life been in Tibet down the centuries that the pictures and the text in accounts by the best of the oldtimers are as up to date as if published last year.

Even if Marco Polo missed out on Tibet, other early Europeans made the grade, some of them even to Lhasa. Our expedition was the last word in luxury compared to the conditions under which those old boys had to travel.

Thinking of the exploits of those seventeenth- and eighteenth-century missionaries and listening to the steady patter of monsoon rains on our bungalow roof we dropped off to sleep. We were confident that a relief crew would appear in the morning, a swarm of willing coolies to help us on to Gangtok.

Next morning came, with a break in the rains, but no coolies. So Dad and I decided to stroll up the road to get a close-up of the slide and figure out what our chances were.

"Maybe," Dad said, "we'll meet a relief party on the other side, or at least be able to round up enough coolies to move our gear across."

It was a sunny, blazing hot morning, and we soon stripped down to our shorts. Without much difficulty we climbed the wall of rock and jungle debris in order to take some pictures and survey the situation. As we clambered on we were alarmed at the number of small stones that were still coming down. Halfway across, we ducked for protection behind a large boulder just in time to avoid a shower of rocks which boomed overhead and bounded down the mountain.

"Whew," Dad said, mopping his brow. "I'm beginning to wonder if we'll ever see Lhasa."

In all our years in the mountains of America we had never encountered landslides the size of this. Obviously we were not in a healthy spot, but since we were halfway over we hustled to the other side of the slide. There we met some of the coolies who had been sent to help us.

From them we learned that we were the first to cross the slide. For weeks afterwards traffic had to detour several miles over the top of the mountain as all loads were transferred to coolies and carried over a jungle track. That night, in Gangtok, we met two other incoming travellers, a Bhutanese prince and his sister. They had been obliged to climb the mountain to get around the avalanche. Even two months later, when we were on our way back from Lhasa, the road was still blocked. However, hundreds of coolies and engineers from Bengal with bulldozers had been at work and, riding in a jeep, we were the first to get through.

Leaving the coolies behind to bring up the gear, we made the final eighteen miles to Gangtok by jeep. It began to drizzle and grew colder as we climbed to the 6,000-foot level, where the Sikkimese capital is located. Shivering in our khaki shorts, we arrived at the mountain-top home of Harishwar Dayal, the Indian political officer. Although we were greeted warmly by Mr. Dayal and his wife—our gracious hosts during our brief stay there—they took one look at our abbreviated costumes and hurriedly supplied us with shirts and coats. They were too polite to express their amazement, but we knew they were thinking what strange people Americans are.

Mr. Dayal had good news for us. Our final clearance for entrance into Tibet had been received. It read in part: "With reference to Mr. Lowell Thomas, United States national, and his son—although the Tibetan government does not usually allow foreign visitors to come to Lhasa—in view of friendly relations between the Tibetan government and the government of the U.S.A., they have granted permission for these two to enter the country." It was signed for the Dalai Lama by Tsipon Shakabpa, the man who headed the first Tibetan trade mission to the United States, in the summer of 1948. We were to meet him later in Lhasa.

With its terraced rice fields and its polyglot population, Gangtok is a colourful town. In spite of its reputation as the tiniest capital in the world, it is one of the most important trade centres on the southern side of the Himalayas. Several caravan routes cross at Gangtok. Its market place is a kaleidoscope of races and costumes. And many tongues are spoken by the Tibetans, Sikkimese, Lepchas, Indians, Sherpas, and Bhutanese who load and unload their pack trains.

Here we met Rinzing Dorje, the swarthy Sikkimese who, for a fat fee and 10 per cent. of the salaries of all persons we hired, organized our caravan for us. A short, fat, jolly fellow with a pigtail wound atop his head, Dorje reminded us of "Chopsticks," the scheming but good-natured Chinese in the comic strip "Terry and the Pirates." Always polite and bowing, Rinzing Dorje proved to be a shrewd operator. Outfitting pack trains was his speciality.

A truly magnificent view of the Potala, " the Palace of the Gods," snapped from the top of nearby Iron Hill. The city of Lhasa proper is out of the limits of this photograph, extending beyond the right side.

On the Roof of the World, as elsewhere, dice games are popular.

Two village women hold offerings for the gods—barley, flour and butter—which they will leave at the *chorten* behind them.

Tibetan nomads, husband and wife.

We found no tractors in the Forbidden Land, and agriculture is where it was centuries ago.

If we found anything puzzling in his accounts, Dorje wasn't embarrassed. He would merely grin and shrug, "If mistake, just subtract!"

In addition to six baggage-carrying coolies, nine pack mules and four riding ponies, Dorje also arranged to hire the rest of the working members of our party. He secured our sirdar, or head-bearer, a Lepcha named Lajor, an invaluable man who could do a little of everything; and two Sikkimese-Tibetans, Tsewong Norbu, a first-rate cook, and Tsewong Namgyal, to fill the vital role of interpreter. Tales of Tibetan travellers are full of the woes that befall those who are unlucky in the servants they hire. But we drew top-flight men for our companions.

Both the cook and the sirdar flaunted wartime United States Army field jackets, G.I. shoes and those knitted caps our troops used to wear under their battle helmets. All through Asia, even in far-off Tibet, you find our surplus army stuff. Even in regions where no G.I. ever penetrated one runs into startling reminders of World War II. In the hinterlands and backwaters, people often wear fantastic combinations of their own colourful and attractive costumes with our leftover military outfits. As for us, on our way through the monsoon belt in the Himalayas, we added to the confusion by wearing rubberized United States Navy storm suits.

During our three days in Gangtok we spent hours in the Dayal courtyard, rearranging supplies and rebuilding the wooden boxes that were made for us in Calcutta. It turned out that they were too big. Each pack animal carries a double load on the trail. And if your boxes are oversize your mule may bang against a mountain wall and go spinning off the narrow trail into canyons thousands of feet below.

At Gangtok, also, we made a batch of recordings with our portable battery-driven recorder. This handy gadget weighs about ten pounds, including batteries, tubes and tiny wrist microphone. Both of us put it to daily use, and it never once failed us throughout the trip. Our spools of recorded tape were rushed across the world to New York and presented as part of Dad's radio news programme— the first on-the-spot broadcasts that had ever been made from the Land of the Lamas.

Finally we were ready. The sirdar, with consideration for healthy appetites, had bought us a slew of tiny tomatoes, potatoes, string beans, eggs and twenty-four loaves of bread. The pack animals, with bells tinkling from their necks, and the coolies, the two Thomases and the rest of the little expedition were set to go. We were off at last on the long caravan journey to the Holy City.

5

OVER THE HIMALAYAN BARRIER

BEFORE we moved on from Gangtok and the hospitable Dayals, the Indian political officer gave us some useful instructions. "Keep in mind that you'll find only a few towns and villages along the way," he said. "You must reach one of these each afternoon. The rest of the time you'll be riding through bleak, empty land. And it's rough going. Every other day or so you'll have to hire a fresh outfit of pack animals."

From Gangtok to the Tibetan capital is usually a trip of twenty-one days. In our eagerness to reach Lhasa, we expected to speed things up and trim five or six days off the schedule. But we reckoned without the mules. No one can drive a mule faster than the critter is willing to move. Besides, the trek to Lhasa is slow and perilous going, over a narrow, twisting, ever-climbing route that often is carved from the perpendicular walls of deep gorges. And the cold, knifelike winds that continually lash the high Tibetan plateau do not make for rapid progress, nor does the rarefied atmosphere of high altitude. We soon learned that fifteen miles a day was a good average for a mule caravan crossing the Himalayas and in Tibet.

On the morning of August 5 we hit the trail on the three-hundred-mile jaunt, first through the rain-soaked forest of Sikkim, then over the towering Himalayas and finally across the windswept Tibetan tableland. There are few trade routes on this globe which have been used as long and as continuously as man has travelled the high road to Lhasa. Those accustomed to four-lane express highways would be hard to convince that the narrow track we were about to follow is one of Tibet's main trade links with the outside world. Stretching back into the dim centuries, caravans have plodded slowly over this sky-line route, bound for India with wool, musk and yak tails. And, winding painfully over the mountains, the traders travel the same route in the same way today.

Our nine pack mules and a half-dozen Sikkimese coolies had started on a few minutes ahead of us, and now from a little distance up the trail echoed the cries of the mule drivers and the dull clank-clank of mule bells.

As we entered the bamboo forest and peered through the drenching monsoon rains into the deep canyon, the whole adventure seemed like a dream. Tsewong Namgyal, our interpreter, smiled and said, "*Kale pe a.*"

"What does that mean?" I asked.

"It's the traditional Tibetan farewell when a caravan sets out to go over the Himalayas," he replied. "It means—go slowly, if you hope to return."

Interpreter Tsewong, riding alongside, told us he had been born in Yatung, Tibet, but that his family had moved to Gangtok when he was young; consequently, he had seen little of his native land. This was to be his first visit to Lhasa. Still in his early twenties, Tsewong had just completed several years of agricultural study at an American missionary college in Allahabad, India, and used our language with some facility. To join up with us he had to do some fast talking with the political officer, because the government had sponsored his education and now expected him to work for Sikkim as an agricultural specialist. As it turned out, we were most fortunate to have his services, for our two servants—Norbu, the cook, and Lajor, our head bearer—while both fine fellows and unrivalled in their own jobs, could speak few words of

English; and interpreting from English to Tibetan and back again was of constant importance to us.

The monsoon rains poured down incessantly as we ambled up the stony trail. Clouds of steam rose from the bamboo jungle and at times made it impossible to see from one end of our procession to the other. These Himalayan foothills have an annual rainfall of 250 inches, second only to the rains of the hills of nearby Assam in volume. So much of that total was emptied on us that we were drenched, despite our rubberized naval storm outfits.

What a contrast between the south and the north side of that Himalayan wall! Jungle on one side; barren mountains and bleak plateau on the other—all because those water-laden clouds, rolling across India from the Bay of Bengal, strike the five-mile-high Himalayas and drop most of their moisture on Sikkim. Since few rain clouds drift beyond the great divide, Tibet has to manage with an average annual rainfall of about twelve inches.

A labyrinth of bamboo and creepers rose straight up over our heads on one side of the narrow trail. On the other side was a sheer drop of thousands of feet. There were many signs of small avalanches, touched off by the tropical downpour.

"I can't help thinking," I said, "what might happen if a landslide like the one we met back in the Tista Valley suddenly caught us here."

"Let's talk about a more pleasant subject," my father suggested.

A more immediate cause for worry was the leeches, tiny blood-suckers, thin as horsehairs and about an inch long. Smelling or sensing the presence of our caravan, they would drop on us from the foliage above and then—if we were not quick to flick them off—loop to an opening in our boots or rain suits. Dad and I were able to keep these pests from fastening to the skin, but our poor coolies were less fortunate and their bare legs bled from leech bites. The mules, too, sneezed miserably with leeches in their nostrils.

Ten miles of stiff climbing brought us to our first dak bungalow, at Karponang. Originally built by the British, the dak bungalows of Sikkim are now maintained by the government of India as shelters for travellers. The one at Karponang is perched in a small clearing near the edge of a gorge at an elevation of ten thousand feet. How pleasant to stretch out before a crackling log fire and dry our dripping clothes!

The next day our caravan swung around some of the higher mountains of Sikkim, over one of the dizziest mountain trails I had ever seen. We looked down into deep chasms, as we rode the ribbon-like trail, too close for comfort to the giddy precipices. Dad's mule persisted in picking her way along the outer edge of the trail—usually within inches of the abyss. His natural impulse was to lean in, an action highly disapproved by the mule and not making her more sure-footed! My own mount had an exasperating way of stopping on the edge of nearly every precipice to reach over for a nibble at some succulent plant. Anyone who thinks he can make mules behave should go to the Himalayas and try his technique on those Sikkimese and Tibetan hardtails!

After another ten miles of slow going and steady climbing (to 12,600 feet) we reached the dak bungalow just above Lake Changu—a calm, dark sheet of water hemmed in by steep slopes covered with rhododendron.

We got off our mules and walked most of the way to Changu, partly because we felt a little safer on our feet than riding along the edge of canyon walls and partly because walking acclimates one more quickly to high altitudes. All day we were gradually climbing out of the bamboo forest, with its steam and leeches, and into terrain similar to that of the American Rockies, with a smattering of pines. We picked wild strawberries from the rocky cliffs—strawberries two and three times the size of American varieties but purple instead of red, and not nearly as sweet. Frequently we stopped to admire the flowers; the beardless purple iris; flat yellow poppies, two inches in diameter; bell-shaped primulas, of which there are some sixty varieties. The mountains of Sikkim at this season were covered with thousands of different flowers, including more than three hundred and fifty varieties of wild orchids and endless varieties of rhododendron. In the Himalayas, incidentally, the rhododendron is a tree, not a bush. Many of these trees grow to a height of thirty and forty feet, with trunks four feet thick. At the miniature end of the scale is the fascinating scarlet dwarf rhododendron.

Here and there we came upon a rather sinister flower, the blue Himalayan monkshood. Into the essence brewed from this poisonous plant, the Sikkimese and Bhutanese, who used to war with each other, would dip their arrows and spears, so that a mere scratch from a weapon caused death. Finally, because so many of their people were related, the Sikkimese and Bhutanese agreed not to use the poison any longer.

Toward the end of this second day's march, we passed acres of yellow daisies that gave off a strange pungent odour. Encountering a Sikkimese on the trail, we were told that any headaches we might have—and we had them —came not from the altitude but from those daisies.

Along the trail danced the loveliest flowers I have ever seen—endless carpets of them, as if nature had lavishly bestowed the ultimate in her adornment of the Himalayas. We were especially enchanted with the Alpine flowers of incredible variety and shades of colour which bordered the trail—some clinging to moss-covered rocks, others glistening like gems on the stumps of dead trees.

"This Himalayan country would be a paradise for a crack botanist. Too bad we don't know more about plants," I said, a bit wistfully. "Why, most of these flowers we've never met up with before."

"Years ago I knew a remarkable Englishman," Father put in, "a chap who devoted his life to hunting orchids and other new species in the Himalayas—Kingdon-Ward. I wish he were with us."

Dad went on to tell me more about Captain Kingdon-Ward. He must be in his middle sixties now, and as far as Dad knows, still makes his headquarters in Calcutta and spends most of his time collecting plant specimens and seeds in the wildest and most inaccessible regions of the Himalayas. In the beginning he had no intention of being a plant collector. Upon graduating from Cambridge, he sailed to Shanghai to teach school. But the call of the wild must have got him when an invitation came from England to collect plants on the Tibetan border of Yunnan. Actually he had studied botany and been brought up on it, for his father—Harry Marshall Ward—had been a distinguished professor of botany at Cambridge University.

"That was about 1910," Dad explained, "when Kingdon-Ward was in his early twenties. He spent two years in the mountains of western China and in south-eastern Tibet. From the wooded highlands east of Lhasa he brought back the famous blue poppy. His first book, about that trip, was called *The Land of the Blue Poppy*—a marvellous account of his experiences as a naturalist and of the aboriginal tribes in mountain country rarely, if ever, visited by Westerners."

From that time on, Kingdon-Ward's career was cut out for him. He was to be a plant hunter in Asia.

"He told me once that plant hunting is a serious business and can be learned only by actual experience," Dad said. "A plant collector working in a mountainous country in search of Alpines has to spend six or seven months in the area selected, from April, when the plants start flowering in the valleys, to November, when the seeds ripen."

OVER THE HIMALAYAN BARRIER

Over the years Kingdon-Ward has roamed the Himalayas in search of plants and has been several times to western China and south-eastern Tibet, to Assam and the north-east frontier of Burma. He has even gone as far afield as Thailand and Indo-China. Out of these many explorations he has created at least a dozen books. Flower lovers may not know that he is responsible for some of the most attractive and unusual flowers now growing in English and American gardens and greenhouses. He has discovered many new varieties of Himalayan and other Asiatic plants, which in the conventional Latin classification of botanists are tagged with his name: "*Wardii*."

"Did he ever get to Lhasa?" I asked.

"Not as far as I know," Dad replied. "But Kingdon-Ward was always more interested in living plants than in living gods."

(Months later, as I sit at home writing about Kingdon-Ward, a press dispatch has come from India saying that he and his wife are missing in the Himalayas of Tibet and Assam, where a stupendous cataclysm of nature has been taking place. For more than a week, the dispatch says, there have been violent earthquakes in those mountains, and scientists believe that on the Roof of the World the face of the earth is being changed. It is not known what has happened to the Kingdon-Wards.

The force of the upheaval has been such that one of the world's major rivers has been thrown from its course. The Brahmaputra, called "Tsangpo" in Tibet, has been hurled into an ancient river-bed—one that it poured through thousands of years ago.

Imagine the floods when a river as big as the Mississippi suddenly alters its course! Sketchy reports from New Delhi state that after a great loss of life ten thousand people are marooned by floods along the wild mountain borders of Assam and Tibet, where the Brahmaputra turns south and begins its prodigious plunge from twelve thousand feet to sea level and the Bay of Bengal. Some two hundred villages have been inundated and their inhabitants forced to take to the treetops to await rescue. The Indian Government has sent a large fleet of shallow-draft boats to navigate the flood waters and save lives. There are grim descriptions of the carcasses of thousands of wild animals—tigers, elephants, and the one-horned rhino—all overwhelmed by the deluge.

The Tibetan sky at night is pictured as having a glow of scarlet. The river waters have turned a sulphury green, like something out of the *Inferno*. Scientists declare that giant Himalayan peaks, which have slept for thousands of years, are bursting forth in volcanic fury.

Geologists believe the quakes will continue for years. They refer to the earthquake of 1897, the worst in modern history, when the shocks in the Himalayas lasted for ten years. This present cataclysm may be just as bad.

A geologist in India points out that the earth's crust has been in motion out there. The Himalayas have grown taller in the past couple of hundred years. Mount Everest, the world's tallest, when calculated some thirty years ago, measured 29,002 feet. Recently Everest measured 29,200 feet—nearly two hundred feet higher. So, based on that, the supposition is that during the present quakes the Himalayas are being thrust up.

If Kingdon-Ward and his wife survive this display of nature's fury, and I have a feeling that they will, what a story they will have to tell the world!)

At Changu that evening, over a hearty dinner of roast beef, beans and potatoes we had an interesting conversation with the Maharaj Kumar of Sikkim, the son of the present Maharaja and next in line to be ruler of that Himalayan state. He happened to drop in at the Changu bungalow while on a fishing trip. The young Sikkimese prince, who speaks flawless English after seven years at a British school in Simla for sons of maharajas, pointed out to us that the blaze on the hearth warming our backs was a rhododendron fire. For heating and cooking, rhododendron is preferred to other kinds of tropical forest timber because it produces greater heat and, most important in a land with a yearly rainfall of from 200 to 250 inches, it will burn even when wet. The Maharaj Kumar and his father, he told us, have been trying to stop their people from cutting down the rhododendron, as a safeguard against denudation. But they have not had much co-operation. A year ago a forest ranger was sent to the Changu region on the trail of poachers who were cutting down rhododendron trees. He caught two of them and was bringing them in for punishment, but he never made it. They pushed him off a precipice—one that we had crossed that afternoon.

It was still raining when we got up next morning, and the beautiful scenic view from Changu was completely shut off. We doggedly set forth through the monsoon downpours. The higher we climbed, the colder it became. For three hours our party wound its way up the mountain. Our mules slipped on the wet stones and slithered through the mud. We passed a Buddhist prayer wheel run by waterpower. It was a barrel ornamented with religious symbols and stuffed with prayers written on cloth and paper. The barrel spun round and round in the rushing stream. With each revolution, it is believed, the prayers are transmitted to Buddha and to the higher gods of the Tibetan spiritual realm.

We were on our way to the border between India and Tibet at Nathu-La (*la* is the Tibetan word for pass). The last few miles before the pass were tedious going, and the rain was cold. To warm up, we hiked the final mile, cutting across the trail—straight up over moss-carpeted rocks through the rhododendron.

Nathu-La, at 14,800 feet, was the highest elevation we had reached as yet. There we encountered none of the military and customs barriers usually found at a frontier.

Three bushy-tailed wild yaks, peering down at us suspiciously from a high ledge before bolting, were the only living things we saw on the Tibet-India border.

Where the trail levelled off and headed into the Forbidden Land, we passed under a yak hair rope fastened to two boulders. From that cord hung hundreds of cloth prayer flags, waving vigorously in the strong wind, each wave carrying the prayers to heavenly headquarters much the same as the revolutions of the water-powered prayer barrel. These flags are essentially good-luck talismans, invoking the aid of such lamaistic deities as the god of wisdom, the protector against accident and illness, and the bestower of long life. Frequently the person making the offering has his name or year of birth inscribed on the flag. And always it carries the mystic syllables which ring constantly from one end of Tibet to the other: *"Om Mani Padme Hum!"* (*Hail to the Jewel in the Lotus!*)

As we crossed the border, we doffed our hats and bowed in accordance with the Tibetan custom. Then, shouting and throwing rocks to frighten away evil spirits, we added our bit to a cairn which had grown to a height of thirty feet as a result of the stone offerings of previous passers-by. Some of the Buddhists in our working party devoutly kept repeating their chant: *"Om Mani Padme Hum!"* *"Om Mani Padme Hum!"* to drive away the demons, who are believed to make their home on Nathu-La, as on all mountain passes.

Lashed by the driving rain, we were too cold to linger at Nathu-La and kept moving on foot down over some washouts into the enormous upper Chumbi Valley.

On the wall to our right and high above, we saw a few patches of snow, from which trickled a ribbon of water that grew larger and larger as it plunged on through the valley. Looking at our maps, we could see that this tiny stream was one of the beginnings of one of the world's mightiest rivers—the Brahmaputra. Halting half a mile down the lee side of the pass we nibbled our lunches of crackers, cheese, and chocolate, washing them down with hot soup and chlorinated water. Our porters also paused for lunch. They pulled small wooden bowls from underneath their garments and partially filled them with white barley flour, which they carried in yak-skin pouches fastened to their belts. Then, adding water from the nearby stream, they kneaded the uncooked mixture into what looked like thick mashed potatoes. Each porter took a bit of this doughlike paste, rolled it into a small ball and ate it with relish. This is *tsamba*, the staple national dish of Tibet. Our porters ate *tsamba* morning, noon and night, mixing it whenever they could with *chang*, Tibetan barley beer. Barley, by the way, is the main crop of Tibet, and almost the only grain that is grown successfully on the Roof of the World.

We continued to walk down the Tibetan side of Nathu-La. In the Himalayas one always dismounts going down any respectable slope, for there's an old Tibetan saying which you are expected to keep in mind: "If he doesn't carry you uphill, he is no horse; and if you don't walk down, you are no man."

The trail now led through a forest of pine and fir, past great patches of Alpine flowers that spread their gay colours in all directions like the waves of a rainbow sea. At last our destination loomed up through the rain, the comfortable and very welcome dak bungalow of Champithong, perched at an elevation of 13,350 feet.

We were over the great Himalayan barrier—inside Tibet at last!

As we shoved off with our caravan next morning, we waved farewell to John Roberts, who had to turn back at this point. He disappeared up the trail with a heavy heart, returning to India with all the tape recordings that we had made thus far.

Dad and I continued down into the Chumbi Valley, bound for Tibet's fourth largest town—Yatung. The sun finally broke through, giving us a wonderful view of the valley, with the Amo River winding past gold and green fields and little villages of white houses. We descended through the forest, where every tree was draped gracefully with a delicate golden moss—not the heavy, almost strangling variety found in our own Deep South.

In the forest we met our first Tibetan monkey. A big white fellow, with a long tail and a black face, which made him look like the old man of the mountains, he sat above us in a pine tree, nonchalantly watching our caravan descend the trail. Tibet is a paradise for chaps like him. Because of their deep-rooted belief in reincarnation, Tibetans avoid killing animals, birds and even fish. If one leads a pure life, he passes on at death to a higher form. If a person behaves badly in this life, he will be demoted in his next. Who knows? That big monkey might have been some Tibetan's scallawag great-great-grandfather! In any case, the Tibetans claimed descent from a monkey centuries before Darwin advanced his theory. According to one of their old chronicles, a monkey, who was an incarnation of Chenrezi, the God of Mercy, met a female demon who was born in misery because of the wickedness of her former life. Out of compassion, the monkey married her. Six children were the result of this union. The father got rid of their tails and long hair by feeding them on sacred grain. And, says the old chronicle, these children were the ancestors of the Tibetans.

On the way to the bottom of the Chumbi Valley, we rounded a bend five or six miles from the top of the pass. Just below, on a rocky ledge, glistened the golden roof of our first Buddhist monastery, Kargyu Gompa—home of a sect of Red Hat monks. The Red Hats do not always practise celibacy. Many marry and have children. They may even have children out of wedlock. Once they ruled Tibet, but today they are in the minority.

As we drew near the turreted, thick-walled building

clinging to the side of the mountain, we could see the monks swarming about the courtyard. Near the entrance an aged priest was sitting on a ledge in the meditative posture of Buddha. He smiled and did not object when we turned our cameras his way. Several monks, led by an abbot in a gold hat, came to the main gate and urged us to stop for the night. We were behind schedule and reluctantly had to decline their invitation. But our one glimpse of that massive stone monastery gave us the feeling that we were indeed in mysterious Tibet.

It would be impossible to venture more than a few miles into Tibet without recognizing the hold that religion and ritual have over the daily lives of all Tibetans. Nearly one-fourth of the males become monks. Although the monks are popularly called lamas by foreigners, the term "lama" is strictly applied only to the incarnate living gods, to the highest clergy and to saintly priests qualified to teach the doctrine. Run-of-the-mill monks are known as *trapa*. The two hundred thousand or more monks are supported in their skyscraping and massive monasteries by the other four million of the population.

The Dalai Lama, assisted by the foremost lamas and abbots and by a handful of noble families, rules the world's last theocracy. No impression of the country and its unique people, centuries removed from the machine-age era, would be complete without some acquaintance with its religion. In view of the distinguished scholars who have devoted their lives to research on the subject, it is temerity on my part to discuss it. But in all humbleness, before travelling farther into Tibet, I shall attempt a brief outline of its religious background.

In the early centuries of the Christian era, the Tibetans were a warlike people, composed of many loosely affiliated tribes. They waged victorious wars, frequently conquering their Central Asian neighbours. Their religion, known as Bön or Pön, was a form of animism. They believed that spirits inhabited the mountains, rocks, lakes, rivers and trees, even the skies above and the earth below. They worshipped the good spirits and tried to placate the evil ones. They resorted to spells, magic and enchantments. In those days there were no monks, no monasteries, no temples. Witchcraft and sorcerers dominated the religious scene.

In the middle of the seventh century, when the various tribes had united, Tibet had a powerful king, Song Tsen Gampo. His armies conquered western China and slices of northern India. Song Tsen Gampo then took as his two chief wives a Chinese princess and the daughter of the King of Nepal. They were both Buddhists. The Chinese princess brought with her a treasured Indian sandalwood image of Buddha. The Nepalese princess also brought as part of her dowry three precious Buddhist images. Working together, the two wives made the king an enthusiastic convert to Buddhism. With the new capital recently established at Lhasa, the two queens desired to erect temples there to enshrine their images. The Chinese queen built the Ramoche temple, still standing and containing a large image of the devout lady. For his Nepalese queen, Song Tsen Gampo himself constructed the famous Jokang, since she was too poor to build a temple. Song Tsen Gampo was a zealous convert and not only gave the first impetus to Buddhism in Tibet, but founded the beginnings of its priesthood. Before the time of this great king Tibet had no written language. Eager to translate the Buddhist scriptures brought from India, he sent one of his ministers to study in India and work out a Tibetan alphabet. Suitable written characters based on Sanskrit models were invented. Song Tsen Gampo is worshipped today as an incarnation of Chenrezi, the patron god of Tibet, the Lord of Mercy, the Avalokitesvara of India, the compassionate Kwanyin of China and Japan.

There are two main divisions of Buddhism: the Hinayana, or Lesser Vehicle; and the Mahayana, or

Using chopsticks as in China, we lunch at the Foreign Office, Lhasa, with five Tibetan statesmen. Mail and papers are " filed," in Tibet, by hanging them in bunches like prayer flags, from walls, pillars and door posts.

Three small-fry relatives of the Dalai Lama pose for us outside the palace. They are, from left to right, Kando Tsiring and Tenzin Ngawang, niece and nephew, and Jizon Pama, the ruler's younger sister.

The narrator of the drama wears a white mask. The dancing, singing and clashing of cymbals throughout the day-long performance are interrupted periodically while he tells the story in a ceremonial chant.

Greater Vehicle. The Hinayana claims to represent the pure teaching of Gautama Buddha, emphasizing the intellectual and rational side, and regarding the Buddha not as a god, but as a great human teacher and sage. The Mahayana puts a more mystical interpretation on the Buddhist doctrine, worships the Buddha as a divine being and offers salvation through faith and love as well as through knowledge. The Hinayana has flourished mainly in South Asia; the Mahayana, in the north.

The comparatively optimistic and easy-going Mahayana Buddhism, introduced into Tibet, with its promise of salvation through faith and not so puritanical or severe in its demands as the older form, gradually appealed to the people. The Bön worshippers and the powerful Bön magicians fiercely fought the spread of Buddhism. But many of the eighth- and ninth-century kings gave it their support. The greatest of these were Ti-song De-tsen and Ralpachan, who combined military conquests with their Buddhism. Together with Song Tsen Gampo, they are worshipped by Tibetans to this day as "The Three Religious Kings, Men of Power." These three kings represented the final period of Tibet as a great military power in Central Asia. As Buddhism gained adherents in Tibet, the martial spirit declined. The late Sir Charles Bell, the eminent British authority on Tibet, was of the opinion that what Tibetans fear most in case of invasion is the loss of their holy religion and that the monks may be expected to fight for this. I quote an interesting passage from his *Religion of Tibet*, published in 1931:

"There are many indications that the martial energy of the Tibetans, though sapped by Buddhism, has not even now been destroyed. Indeed, Tibet expects to fight later on for her religion. You can sometimes read in Tibetan books about the country called Shambhala. When people talk about it they usually call it 'Shambhala of the North,' and describe it as a mystical country which, three or four centuries hence, will be the scene of hostilities, fierce and decisive. One sees paintings representing the battle in Tibetan houses. Bodhisattvas are depicted as joining in the fray; in fact it is they who decide it. Shambhala lies somewhere to the north-west of Tibet. Dorjieff, the influential Mongol from Russian Mongolia, who used to hold a Chair of Philosophy at Lhasa, claimed that Shambhala is Russia."

Under Ti-song De-tsen the celebrated Tantric teacher, Padma Sambhava, "The Lotus Born," was brought from India. He was believed to have occult powers to subdue evil spirits and demons. Tantrism, with its magic formulas and miracles, appealed strongly to the Tibetan masses, steeped in their old nature worship and fear of demons. Padma Sambhava founded the first large monastery in Tibet in A.D. 777 at Samye, a few miles south-east of Lhasa. The Tantric Buddhism taught by Padma Sambhava was combined with features of the original Bön cult and developed into lamaism. The Red Hat sect, followers of the early Buddhism of Tibet, revere him as their chief saint.

Although Buddhism is practically extinct today in India, it was at that time the fountain of inspiration for all Buddhist countries. Many Indian holy men and sages, especially from northern India, where Tantrism flourished, were invited to Tibet to spread their teaching. Tibetan monks likewise went to India to study at the feet of the masters and faithfully copy the old Buddhist scriptures into Tibetan. The tropical climate of India was almost unbearable for the Tibetans, accustomed to their cold, invigorating highlands. Many died, but a few returned with their precious translations. The scholarly monks of Sakya compiled the first authoritative edition of the Tibetan Buddhist Canon. The *Kangyur*, the Tibetan Bible, is in 108 volumes; the *Tengyur*, or Commentaries, in 225 volumes. So faithful are the Tibetan translations to the

Sanskrit originals, many of which were lost or destroyed in India, that Buddhist scholars today make every effort to gain permission to study rare treasures in the libraries of Tibetan monasteries.

The Red Hats held sway for several centuries. But with increased riches they became indifferent to their duties and introduced unsavoury practices which repelled some of the higher-minded among the clergy. At this period, in the middle of the fourteenth century, Tibet's greatest religious reformer, Tsong-kapa—The Man from the Land of Onions —was born in the province of Amdo, near the Chinese border. He had his monastic training at Sakya and was determined to revive the religion in a purer form. His priests were celibate, abstained from wine, and were expected to lead simple and devout lives. He abolished the more extravagant and sensual Tantras, preserving only the esoteric teachings of the Tantric school. Tsong-kapa founded Ganden monastery near Lhasa, to this day the third largest in all Tibet. The reformed sect was called Gelugpa—the Virtuous Way. Popularly, its followers were known as Yellow Hats, from the yellow hoods they wore, in contrast to the unreformed Red Hats. After some setbacks and conflicts with the Red Hats, the Yellow Hats finally gained the supremacy, which they hold to this day. A dwindling number of Red Hats still have their own monasteries and sometimes they may be found dwelling amicably in cloistered peace with the Yellow Hats.

The great reformer's successor, the son of a herdsman, founded the Tashi Lhunpo monastery—The Mount of Blessing—which was seven years in the building. He had a reputation far and wide for his saintliness. Unfortunately we did not see this monastery, near Shigatse, since it was two hundred miles west of Lhasa and off our direct route to the capital. It is the traditional seat of the Panchen Lama—the Panchen Rimpoche—as the Tibetans call him. The Panchen Lama is second in rank to the Dalai Lama, and in spiritual matters often considered his equal. But the Dalai Lama rules both in religious and temporal matters. Actually, nobody challenges any decisions of the god-king in Lhasa. There has been no incarnation of the Panchen Lama at Tashi Lhunpo since 1924, when that living god fled to China because of a serious breach with the thirteenth Dalai Lama. The self-exiled Panchen Lama died in 1937. The Chinese Communists recently got hold of a twelve-year-old Tibetan in north-west China, and they have been pushing him forward as the reincarnation of the late Panchen Lama. The Chinese Reds have been trying to use the boy to stir up revolt in Tibet.

For the long and intricate account of the development of lamaism, the interested reader may turn to a number of authoritative books. Later on, in talks with everyday Tibetans, in our meeting with the Dalai Lama and others close to him, and in visits to the monasteries, I shall try to show something of the religion in present-day Tibetan life as my father and I observed it.

6

THE DALAI LAMA'S PASSPORT

LEAVING the Red Hat Monastery we descended through a forest of fir trees. On the way to Yatung, we forded the swift, roaring Amo River, the first of the many tributaries of the Brahmaputra that we were to cross. Here again were many tall poles with prayer flags snapping in the wind. A little farther on we passed a number of pagoda-like stone structures called *chortens*, roadside religious shrines found near every Tibetan village and often containing sacred relics and images. Another common roadside shrine is the *mani*, or prayer wall. Everywhere along the road to Lhasa, especially at the approach to a village or a monastery, the traveller encounters these low walls, built of masonry and cement, into which stones have been inserted, carved with sacred texts, usually the favourite *Om Mani Padme Hum*. These walls often extend for a quarter of a mile or more. Pious Tibetans add to the walls and to the inscriptions to pile up Buddhist merit for themselves. Prayer walls, *chortens*, monasteries, all hallowed objects, places, and even exalted persons must be passed so that they are on your right, as a sign of respect. The Tibetans have a proverb: "Beware of the devils on the left-hand side."

On the outskirts of Yatung I was startled when a young Chinese wearing black riding boots, a white sweater and broad-brimmed ten-gallon hat addressed me in perfect English: "Hello there, where are you going?"

I learned from him that he was one of the Chinese who,

as I explained in an earlier chapter, were being tossed out of Tibet, chiefly to give concrete evidence of Tibetan independence of Chinese or foreign influence. He was on his way to China. There were, I discovered, between fifty and sixty Chinese in Yatung, all fugitives from Lhasa.

"How many Chinese are being ordered to leave Tibet?" I asked him.

"All who are not traders," he replied.

"What are you?"

"I'm a trader."

"What do you trade in?"

"Oh, wool and other things."

"If you are a trader, why must you leave?"

"I don't know." He seemed ill at ease and forced a laugh. (Later on we learned that he had been working in the Tibetan Government.)

"Where did you learn to speak such good English?"

Again he seemed disconcerted. "Oh, let's say I learned in India."

Subsequently we were told that he came originally from Inner Mongolia, which is attached to Soviet Siberia, and that he had spent five or six years studying in Japan.

Yatung is in a valley so deep that the sun does not appear until just before noon and is gone again three hours later. But with its colourful main street along the Amo, its orchards and flowers, and its snarling mastiffs, Tibet's fourth city is far less dismal than one would expect. It is a lively trading centre and many of its residents are comparatively prosperous.

After our meeting with the Chinese, our pack train continued through the cobbled streets to a charming house of log structure, the home of the Indian trade agent. Standing at the gate to greet us was a smiling Sikkimese in long, flowing robes—our genial English-speaking host, the Rai Bahadur Sonam.

THE DALAI LAMA'S PASSPORT

During dinner that evening at his home, conversation turned to the Tibetan attitude toward outsiders.

The Rai Bahadur told us that Tibet has no desire to change; the people want their way of life to continue unaltered. They think that foreigners have little to offer them and, in fact, can have only a corrupting influence. According to our host, the process of getting on in a modern country seems one awful "rat race." The Tibetan wants no part in it; he wants to be shut off from the madness of the outside world and left alone in his mountains, where he can follow the good life of a Buddhist. This, he believes, will eventually free him from the cycle of reincarnation and deliver him into the Buddhist spiritual world—into Nirvana.

In Tibet the emphasis is on the spiritual rather than on the temporal. Tibetans cannot be blamed for trying to preserve the way of life that suits them. Perhaps they have the answer. Perhaps it would be a good thing for the world if, as the Rai Bahadur put it, Tibet were left "the one nation where life might continue unchanged from that of the earliest times."

However, present-day obstacles may blast such a dream —notably Russia, of which our Yatung host said: "It wants to meddle with every country's affairs, even with those of Tibet." We wondered if it could any longer be possible for a nation, no matter how remote, no matter how isolated by high mountains, to shut itself off from the problems of the world, especially in this age of high speed, high-flying planes, radio short wave, and atomic energy.

To secure our Tibetan passport—the *lamyik*—the Rai Bahadur Sonam introduced us to the local Tibetan trade agent, the Tromo Trochi of Dhomu. He appeared in official dress—a full-length blue robe wound with a red sash. His dark pigtail was coiled atop his head, and from his left ear dangled a four-inch pendant of turquoise, pearl and gold. All this was crowned by a Western fedora!

(The one thing Western about which Tibetans are enthusiastic is the felt hat.)

Arriving with this impressive gentleman were three servants bearing gifts. One carried a tray piled with eggs —a hundred or more of them—some fresh, some ancient. In lamaland, as in China, they like them both ways. The next servant had a large shoulder of yak, all butchered and dressed. The third held a big bowl of yak butter. All these gifts were much appreciated, especially by our servants, who used the rancid yak butter for their all-important yak-butter tea, the national drink of Tibet.

As the Tromo Trochi of Dhomu approached, he alternately stuck out his tongue and hissed at us. These gestures are marks of good manners and proper etiquette on the Roof of the World. As we offered to shake hands with him, he passed a white silk scarf or *kata* over our outstretched arms. This was our first experience with the novel Tibetan way of welcoming a visitor.

We returned his courtesy by presenting him with a similar scarf from the supply we had brought from Sikkim. Then, from our box of gifts we selected a gold-plated automatic pencil which could be adjusted to write in four colours and we gave it to him as our present to the Dalai Lama's agent. Between sips of tea, he hissed politely at us to indicate approval of what we told him through our English-speaking host.

The agent bestowed an unusual honour upon us by inscribing some Tibetan characters on our two American passports and stamping them with the ancient seal of the Lhasa government. We were told that this was the first time any passport had been so endorsed. What the Tromo Trochi wrote may be translated as follows:

"Mr. Lowell Thomas, American citizen, has been permitted to visit Lhasa by the Tibetan government. Sealed by the Tromo Trochi of Dhomu; dated the seventeenth day of the Tibetan sixth month of the Earth Bull year."

THE DALAI LAMA'S PASSPORT

Tibet has worked out a unique calendar which has been in operation for a thousand years. Five elements are combined with twelve animals to designate the years. Every sixty years there is a complete cycle. The elements are earth, iron, water, wood and fire, and each element comes twice, first as male and then as female. The twelve animals—dog, pig, mouse, ox, tiger, hare, dragon, serpent, horse, sheep, monkey and bird—change every year. Thus 1949 was the year of the Earth Bull; 1950 is the year of the Earth Female Tiger; 1951, the Iron Male Hare Year.

Yatung marked the end of the line for our Sikkimese mule train. There both the men and mules that had served us across Nathu-La turned back to Gangtok. Now we had to line up a new Tibetan pack train for the next leg of our journey—a two-day march to the town of Phari.

The next morning we woke up to find our new transportation ready and waiting to load up. There were sixteen pack animals to carry our thirty-seven boxes of supplies, and five riding mules. From now on all our servants would ride too, Norbu, the cook, and Lajor, our bearer, as well as interpreter Tsewong. But before we could get away, we had to await the arrival of the *lamyik*, the document without which the traveller cannot proceed any farther inside Tibet.

Shortly after breakfast the Tromo Trochi brought us this Tibetan passport. It had been written with a bamboo pen in the Tibetan script, which looks like Sanskrit, on a piece of parchment measuring two by three feet. We gathered round as the Tromo Trochi opened up this scroll. Tsewong translated it for us:

"From Dhomu [Yatung] right up to Lhasa, let it be known to all dzongs [officials] and to all others that a message has been received from the Tibetan Government that two Americans, with an interpreter and servants, have permission to proceed to Lhasa. And that sixteen pack mules and six riding animals be given to them, and coolies if required. Accounts for transport are to be settled by their armed escort, Chogpon Nima Gyabu, at the local rate. On the route, preparation for lodging, servants for the kitchen, skin boats to cross rivers and any other requirements such as milk, eggs and vegetables are to be given to them at the current rate. The wishes of the two Americans are to be fulfilled at a moment's notice. For this journey let them be given everything without fail, as Americans are very good friends of Tibet. If they wish to proceed forthwith after arrival at each stage of the journey, let their wishes be gratified."

When the Dalai Lama's passport was spread out before us, I could not help thinking that many Western explorers who had failed to reach Lhasa would have highly prized a document like this, guaranteeing safe conduct and the authority to procure supplies on the high road to the capital.

Take W. Woodville Rockhill, who had a distinguished career as an American diplomat until his death in Honolulu on his way back to China in 1914. He had been United States Minister to China, and to several Balkan states, Ambassador to Russia and to Turkey, and he occupied a number of other important posts. As an Orientalist and specialist on Tibet his work is still highly regarded. From the time he was a boy he had been much interested in Tibetan Buddhism. As a young secretary of our legation in Peiping he devoted himself to a study of the Chinese and Tibetan languages. He was fluent in both. It was his heart's desire to explore unknown regions of Tibet and, above all, to visit Lhasa. So in 1888 Rockhill resigned his position in the diplomatic service and set out in December from Peiping by way of Koko Nor, reaching the Tsaidam basin in the border region the following spring. He dressed and lived like a Chinese frontiersman, a Mongol or Tibetan. By April he was well over the high ranges inside Tibet on his way to the capital. He had started out with sixty pounds of silver and twenty pounds of gold sewed in his clothing. But now his money was giving out, and also his animals and guides and provisions. So he had to abandon the road to Lhasa and turn south-east through the Kham country and back to China.

He confessed, "I nearly starved to death; time and again I was snow-blind; I had to run for my life before the hostile lamas of eastern Tibet; and I vowed I would never go on another such fool's errand."

But not even a year passed before Rockhill was again making arrangements to try his luck in the wilds of Tibet, push through to Lhasa and cross into India. He was only about one hundred miles from the capital when he was ordered to go back.

Unfortunately, Rockhill never realized his ambition to see the Holy City. But his journeys into Tibet proved of real value to science. In addition to his descriptions of hitherto unknown nomad and mountain tribes, he carefully surveyed some three thousand five hundred miles, crossed sixty-nine passes, took sextant observation at one hundred points, and collected from three to four hundred ethnological, botanical and geological specimens.

Then there was Dr. Sven Hedin, the eminent Swedish explorer of Central Asia and Tibet, who made his first journey into Tibet only a few years later than Rockhill and, like the American, had a burning desire to reach Lhasa. How he would have prized our passport! In the summer of 1896 Hedin established headquarters north-west of Tibet in the oasis of Khotan in the vast Takla Makan desert of Chinese Turkistan, now Sinkiang. In this pleasant oasis he assembled his caravan. They crossed over the high passes to the crest of the vast northern Tibetan plateau and plunged forward in the face of violent gales, hailstorms, snow blizzards and cutting winds.

On those bleak northern plains they did not meet a single human being for fifty-five days. Pasturage became more and more scarce, and one by one the animals collapsed and died. The food was nearly gone when they finally came into a valley where a group of Mongols were grazing their yak herds. Only three camels, three horses and one donkey remained of all the animals that had set forth so bravely. The expedition rested a few days with the friendly Mongols, who sold them horses and provisions.

Freshly equipped and in much better spirits, they continued steadily to the east. After crossing the half-frozen Yak River, the caravan came into sight of Koko Nor (the Blue Lake), which, Hedin said, "shifted from one glorious malachite-green shade to another."

It was November, too late to attempt the journey south over treacherous passes to Lhasa. And Sven Hedin, who had by this time spent four years exploring other unknown regions of Central Asia, as well as northern Tibet, was a bit short of funds. He paid off his caravan at the Chinese frontier and went on to Peiping and Europe. The main result of his first Tibetan journey was the discovery of a chain of twenty-three lakes which Hedin incorporated into the map of Asia. He now knew the kind of obstacles which lay ahead of him in Tibet. "I had learned that Tibet is one of the most difficult countries on earth to conquer for purposes of human research and knowledge."

But obstacles never fazed the famous Swedish explorer. He was determined to push through to Lhasa, which had been seen by no European since the visit made by the French Lazarist fathers, Huc and Gabet, in 1846. Young, enthusiastic and triumphant from his sensational discovery of the ancient buried city of Lou-lan in the desert region of Central Asia, his appetite was now whetted for a second adventure in Tibet. In 1901 he tried again, enduring many perils, only to be turned back by polite but determined officials.

Tibet lured Hedin a third time—in 1906. His interest in Lhasa had waned, since the British Younghusband Expedi-

76

tion had already marched into the Forbidden City. Hedin was an explorer who collected trophies of firsts, not seconds or thirds. What intrigued him now were the large white spots on the map of Tibet, especially the country north of the Tsangpo, or upper Brahmaputra. With a splendidly equipped expedition, carrying all the scientific instruments needed for his studies, Hedin started for Tibet by way of Leh and the 17,600-foot Chang-La. During his two years in Tibet, he discovered the sources of two of the holy rivers of India, the Brahmaputra and the Indus. He mapped much of Chang Tang, the empty, desolate northern plain, and made soundings and measurements of unknown lakes. That he was continually pursued by Tibetan officials was an advantage in a way, since it gave him the chance to cross eight times by eight different passes the great range of mountains to which he gave the name "Transhimalaya." It was a remarkable achievement, leading to many important discoveries. And as a consolation prize for never reaching Lhasa, he spent six weeks at Tashi Lhunpo as the personal guest of the Panchen Lama—the number-two living god of Tibet!

One might assume that Sven Hedin would have been prematurely broken in health by the many hairbreadth escapes, privations and sufferings he endured in the desert and in Tibet. Instead, it seems to have given him an extra lease on life. He celebrated his eighty-fifth birthday in Stockholm in February, 1950, and he is still busily working away on the final volumes of the mammoth scientific report dealing with his Central Asian discoveries. He alienated many of his old friends and colleagues by his vociferous support of Germany in both world wars, but his regrettable political views can hardly detract from his reputation as one of the great explorers of modern times.

7

BRITAIN AND TIBET

In accordance with our passport, we were to have, as our official guide for the remaining 250 miles from Yatung to Lhasa, Chogpon (Corporal) Nima Gyabu of the Tibetan army. He carried the all-important passport in his yak-skin saddle bag. Perched atop his gaily bedecked mule, the corporal led the way along the banks of the roaring Amo. Slung across his back was a Springfield clip rifle, with a bit of red yak cloth in the tip of the barrel; and on his hip he carried a portable altar, his silver prayer box containing an image of Buddha. With his long black pigtail dancing to and fro across his rifle and prayer box, the Chogpon set a lively pace, as the many bells attached to his mule echoed through the valley.

Along the route we were now travelling runs the only combination telephone-telegraph wire linking Lhasa with Gangtok and the outside world. Originally strung up by the British, it is often put out of commission by storms and high winds. When it was first built, nomads would rip down sections of the wire for their own use. After the penalty for this became known—forfeiture of a hand— few man-made interruptions cut communications on that lone line to Lhasa.

That day we climbed slowly from Yatung for twelve miles to an altitude of 13,500 feet. For the first time we could really enjoy the magnificent scenery around and below us, since most of the heavy mist of our earlier marches through the rain and monsoon had cleared away.

We kept close to the rushing Amo, with its many falls and cataracts churning the pale green water into milky froth. I was reminded of a trip I made a few years ago in the Canadian Rockies. Then I packed on horseback into the mountains west of Banff, travelling with a Norwegian ski friend, Erling Strom, to his camp at the foot of Mount Assiniboine. We rode through the same sort of pine forest, along the same kind of mountain stream as the Amo. The chief difference was that here in southern Tibet we were continually meeting wool-bearing yak caravans; in the Rockies the moose peered out at us through the timber.

On our sixth day of travel into the breath-taking vastness of the Himalayas, we climbed for about seven miles along the mountain wall, up and up, until we came to the great Central Asian plateau. Then another seven miles or so across the highest plain I had ever seen. All that afternoon we rode at an altitude of more than fourteen thousand feet, higher than the tallest peaks in our American Rockies. On those high Tibetan trails, there is no danger of suddenly rounding a corner and running into a car or even a cart; there are no shrieking horns, only the pleasant tinkle of caravan bells.

Others who have taken the Tibetan highroad have complained of gasping for breath, dizziness, nausea and inability to sleep except when sitting up. But we were not troubled by the mountain sickness that plagues many who climb great heights. Perhaps our frequent ski trips back home and our strenuous exercise at fairly high altitudes were responsible for our immunity.

Jogging along on our mules at about 14,500 feet, we were surrounded by mountain peaks rising another three to six thousand feet above us.

Dad turned to me. "How would you like to take off down those slopes on your skis?"

"I was just thinking it would be great sport," I agreed. "I'll bet there's room up there for all the twenty million skiers in the world to come schussing down at once without anybody having to yell 'track.' "

As we wound out of the gorges of the Amo and emerged on the great plateau, our caravan dismounted. We had come to a sinister place and stopped to appease the demons. At that point were two *chortens*. The larger one, across the valley from us, contained a copper urn. Many years ago when the *chorten* was built and people still clung fearfully to the old Bön superstitions and rites, blood was poured into the urn. A boy and a girl, each eight years old, were sacrificed and their bodies placed in it. A demon must have smelled the blood and corpses, the Tibetans told us. The evil spirit took over and made that neighbourhood dangerous for human beings. To counteract the demon's evil influence another *chorten* was built on our side of the valley. Here our whole party offered prayers to Buddha and left money for the monk who presides at the spot. Although our mule train crossed the Himalayas with the Dalai Lama's blessing and we punctiliously stopped at every mountain pass, river and *chorten* to pay our respects to the spirits who are supposed to have dwelt there since the dawn of time, perhaps we did not appease them sufficiently. They certainly got their revenge on the American intruders. When Dad had his hip shattered in eight places on the homeward trek, I wondered if the demons of sacred Chomolhari and the other mountains of snow and ice were chortling. Or was it something more subtle they had in mind? Was the accident their way of drawing attention to a danger threatening Tibet?

That same day on the plain we saw our first large herd of yak. What an animal! Without him I doubt if there could be a Tibet. A distant relative of the American buffalo, this shaggy, sure-footed critter serves a multitude of purposes. Easily domesticated, the yak forages for himself by snipping off sparse grass and coarse, thorny herbage with his long, barbed tongue. The yak is thus an ideal beast of burden in that lofty, windswept land. Although he moves slowly, and rarely covers more than nine miles a day, he carries heavy burdens and is unfalteringly steady-footed on the steepest and most dangerous trails.

This accommodating beast helps also to plough the fields and flail the barley. He yields an almost indestructible wool for the tents of nomads. Boots are made of yak cloth and yak leather, and a suit of yak cloth lasts a lifetime. All rope in Tibet is woven from yak hair. The hide furnishes leather which is used for innumerable purposes, including the building of skin boats. Yak horns and bones are utilized in building houses and walls. Even yak tails are famous. In Asia they are prized as fly whisks, and from those shipped to America we make nearly all of our better Santa Claus beards. Most indispensable is dried yak dung, the fuel of most of Tibet, which mines no coal and has almost no wood.

Finally, and most important, the yak provides milk, butter and meat, which, with tea and *tsamba*, are staples of Tibetan diet. It may seem inconsistent that the Tibetans are great eaters of meat—mutton as well as yak—in view of the Buddhist aversion to the killing of all life, animal as well as human. But the severe climate and the strenuous, outdoor life of the Tibetans demands a meat diet, whenever it can be afforded. On several holy days of the month it is forbidden to butcher yak or sheep. For butchering, special places are set aside. Usually yaks are slaughtered by suffocation, to keep the blood in the meat. The butchers and others who kill animals for food realize that they are committing a great sin, due to wickedness in their previous lives, and the Tibetan Buddhist books condemn the practice in no uncertain terms. The shepherds and herdsmen on the plains, however, don't worry their heads much about the matter.

Here and there in the distance we spotted the black yak

hair tents of the shepherds, reminding us that Tibet is a land of nomads, as well as of great, forbidding lamaseries and of one famous city, as difficult to enter as Ali Baba's cave without the magic words.

Our next stop was Phari, a collection of stone and sod houses, which has been unanimously described by travellers as "the highest, windiest, dirtiest town in the world"— an opinion with which we were heartily inclined to agree.

Most Tibetans are short, sturdy folk. Although their origin is uncertain, they are generally believed to be partly of Mongolian and partly of Burmese and Assamese descent. Their language belongs to the same family as Burmese. With high cheekbones, straight black hair, coppery skins and merry eyes, they are not unlike our Navajo Indians in physical appearance. But the residents of Phari seemed dirtier than the Tibetans we met elsewhere. Their costumes were colourless, drab, greasy and smudged from yak-dung smoke. The longer a Tibetan lived in Phari the darker his complexion got, apparently because more dirt had worked its way into his skin. Phari folks did not seem disturbed that water rarely touched their bodies. The layers of dirt are a protection against the winds that forever blast across the Phari plain, especially in the winter.

And the streets of Phari! Piled high with the dirt and garbage of centuries, it was almost impossible to pick one's way through the muck. It seems quite appropriate that the translation of Phari is "Hog Hill." If Phari has the reputation of being the dirtiest town in the world, it may also boast of having the world's loftiest post office at an altitude of 14,700 feet.

We were welcomed to Phari by the Tibetan district governor, Rimshi Dote, a man towering to almost seven feet, the tallest person we met in Tibet. In addition to two white scarves, Rimshi Dote presented us with a large sack of barley and a butchered lamb. The high spot in our sojourn at Phari was an evening with the governor and his wife. In their charming oriental home, close by our dak bungalow, we sat with the Rimshi Dotes on Tibetan leopard skins and sipped our first yak-butter tea, which was not at all bad.

Tea à la Tibet is considered exceptionally nutritious and is one of the mainstays of the Tibetan diet. Usually it is made by the young ladies of the household. In a wooden cylinder about three feet high with a bore three inches in diameter, they churn the tea with a wooden stick. The ingredients of this popular Tibetan drink are boiling water, soda (from the lakes of Tibet), tea from China, and large gobs of yak butter, preferably rancid. The whole mixture is stirred and mashed together in the wooden cylinder until it takes on the consistency and appearance of a heavy soup or thick gravy.

Soon after tea the Rimshi of Phari invited us to sit down to a sumptuous feast. We were beginning to learn that, although the common man of Tibet lives on barley flour and buttered tea, members of the nobility—those two hundred all-powerful families—eat China's finest. That evening we had countless courses—several varieties of vegetables and meat, including yak's liver and tongue, noodle soup and fresh fruit from the neighbouring state of Bhutan. We managed as best we could with ivory chopsticks, and joined in the merriment created by our awkward but well-meaning efforts. We were interested to hear from Rimshi Dote that he was the man who early in the war rescued the five United States fliers who had to bale out of their bomber in a remote corner of Tibet.

The crack-up of the American fliers in Tibet was quite an experience for lads from Indiana, Massachusetts, Oklahoma, Texas and Rockville Centre, Long Island—two lieutenants, two corporals and a private first class. They were returning, at night, to their home base in India after flying supplies over the Hump to China. The high

Himalayan peaks were hidden in a thick pea-soup fog. Once in a rift through the heavy clouds they saw lights and assumed they were over an Indian city. They circled it, trying to signal the radio tower, but they had no answer. Obviously not. There was no airfield. With their gas gone and barely a second to spare, they parachuted down into the darkness. Landing on rocky cliffs, they were pretty badly bruised and slashed and even acquired a broken arm or two. They saw they were near a big river. They took it for the Brahmaputra, and they were right. Only they were not in the Assam valley, as they thought.

In the morning, dazed and shattered, the five brave fliers stumbled for two days along the river bank until they came to a town. One of the pilots spoke a bit of Hindustani and one of the villagers spoke a little, too. The flabbergasted fliers discovered they were in Tibet, in the town of Tsetang, not far from Lhasa, over which they had flown the first aeroplane in history to soar above the Holy City. Friendly and hospitable, the villagers lodged them, fed them strange food, plied them with *chang*, the Tibetan barley beer, fussed over them and were as curious about them as if they had come from another planet. Their hosts, however, gave them no hope of getting out, with the mountain passes closed by December snows and bandits loose in the hills.

But news travels quickly in Tibet, even without telephones. In a short time a Sikkimese doctor from the British Political Office came to take them to Lhasa, but not before their village friends turned out to give them blankets, fur robes, fur-lined boots and a grand send-off. Even the residents of Lhasa were friendly and did not seem to resent the flight over the Dalai Lama's city, sacrilegious as it was. The stranded airmen spent five days at the British Government House, where they were royally entertained and provided with all the comforts of home by British Major Sherriff and his wife.

BRITAIN AND TIBET

The fliers were well treated because the Tibetan officials realized that America has no ulterior or hostile designs on their country. All the same, the crew of the wrecked plane was hustled out of Tibet as expeditiously as possible. The Tibetans want to have as little as possible to do with the outside world. It is the wish of their rulers that everything remain as it was centuries ago.

The squalor of Phari is somewhat redeemed by the medieval splendour of the Dzong—the old fort—with its thick stone walls and narrow slits of windows. Built on higher ground than the surrounding plain, the Dzong dominates for miles the whole scene as well as the little town clustered beneath it.

Not far from here the Younghusband Expedition defeated a Tibetan army in 1904. But the story of that conflict and what led up to it will require a backward glimpse of some years into the relations of Tibet with the British Raj in India.

Warren Hastings, the first governor general of India under the British Raj, tried to open trade relations and neighbourly communications between India and Tibet in 1774. He selected George Bogle, a tactful, affable, clever young man on the staff of the East India Company, to undertake the mission. Entering Tibet by way of Bhutan, Bogle took the same route we were now following through the Chumbi Valley and Phari as far as Gyantse. His objective was an interview with the Panchen Lama. Learning that his Tibetan Holiness had not been at his Tashi Lhunpo monastery in Shigatse for three years because of a serious smallpox epidemic, Bogle turned north-east and crossed the Tsangpo to a small town not very far from Lhasa, where the Panchen Lama was temporarily residing. Bogle was received "in the most engaging manner" by the great Lama, who treated the young Englishman without ceremony after a few official visits. Indeed, they struck up a warm friendship.

When the Panchen Lama returned a month later to Tashi Lhunpo, Bogle was urged to come, too, and given quarters near the living god. He met many important Tibetans, and everything was progressing beautifully. But in Lhasa the Dalai Lama was an infant and the Regent, hostile to *pilingi* (Europeans), insisted that the Panchen Lama find some excuse to get rid of Bogle. On his return to India Bogle kept up a cordial correspondence with the Panchen Lama. Before Bogle could arrange for further negotiations with Tibet, his friend the Panchen Lama died in Peiping of smallpox, and Bogle himself died in Calcutta not long afterward.

In the early nineteenth century a number of adventurous Englishmen undertook trips to Tibet on their own. Among them was Thomas Manning, an eccentric chap who had few friends except for the famous Lambs, Charles and Mary. His passion was the study of the Chinese language. After living three years among the Chinese in Canton, he took a notion that he would like to visit Tibet. Dressed in Chinese clothes and accompanied by his Chinese servant, he got as far as Phari, where he was discovered and detained. But his rudimentary knowledge of medicine proved helpful. At Phari he met a Chinese general and successfully treated some of the soldiers of his escort. The grateful general took him on to Gyantse and even wrote to Lhasa, asking permission for Manning to continue on to the capital. Surprisingly enough, the permission came. In December, 1811, Manning entered Lhasa, and was hospitably received by the authorities. His meagre knowledge of medicine, which he practised busily, and his unofficial standing made him a welcome guest. He was even presented to the Dalai Lama, then seven years of age.

Manning stayed four months in Lhasa; not having Bogle's warmth of personality or keen gift for reporting, he could not make full use of his unusual opportunity. It was unfortunate, since he was the first Englishman ever to visit Lhasa and the first European to enter the capital since the expulsion of the Capuchin friars in 1745. He sailed for England soon after his return to India, and seemed content to spend the rest of his life quietly at home after his one great adventure.

About the same time that Manning made his journey to Lhasa, Thomas Moorcroft of the Indian Civil Service obtained permission from the Indian Government to cross the Himalayas into western Tibet with two objectives in mind: first, to obtain samples of the wool from which the Cashmere shawls were made, and second, to survey the country surrounding Mount Kailas and sacred Lake Manasarowar at the foot of the holy mountain. Disguised as a merchant and with no intention of pushing east to the capital, he had no difficulty. Twelve years later, again disguised as a merchant, he went on another exploring trip accompanied by a German named Trebeck. In 1825 Trebeck reported that Moorcroft had died somewhere along the road to Bokhara. But when the famous traveller Abbé Huc was in Lhasa in 1846, he was told that a foreigner named Moorcroft had come to the capital in 1826, dressed as a Moslem. Huc had never even heard of Moorcroft before, so the story is plausible. Speaking Urdu —the Persian-Indian dialect—fluently, Moorcroft had even deceived the Kashmiri Moslem merchants of Lhasa among whom he lived. For the purpose of inspecting herds he was buying, Moorcroft went about the country freely, making drawings and geographical charts.

After twelve years in Lhasa, Moorcroft set out for Ladakh and India, but on the way he was killed by bandits. The Lhasa authorities arrested the robbers and, recovering Moorcroft's possessions, found his plans and maps. From this evidence the Tibetans concluded that they had harboured a dangerous foreigner in the very heart of the Holy City. Unfamiliar with modern science, the Tibetans could not understand the eagerness of foreigners to explore and map their country except for sinister purposes of future conquest. Hence, they became increasingly suspicious and distrustful of all Europeans attempting to journey into Tibet.

Although the British in India disclaimed any intention of conquest, they had an avid scientific and geographical interest in accurately filling in the many blank spaces on the map of the forbidden country to the north of the Himalayan barrier. It was decided to train and employ intelligent natives of the upper Himalayas, preferably those speaking both Hindustani and Tibetan, to make secret map surveys in Tibet. Under the skilful direction of Colonel T. G. Montgomerie and, after his death, under Captain (later General) Henry Trotter, several men were trained at Dehra Dun in technical exploration work, such as taking compass bearings, observing for latitude, making boiling-point records for altitude and recognizing the more important stars.

The native explorers travelled in disguise as pious pilgrims. Equipped with the commonly used hand prayer wheel, a hollow copper box, cylinder-shaped, revolving around a spindle, the surveyor substituted for the prayers long strips of blank paper on which he could note his bearings and observations. He carried a rosary made up with one hundred beads instead of the 108 required by Buddhist ritual, and each tenth bead a little larger than the others to make it convenient to count off the distances by one hundred or one thousand paces. Latitudes were taken with a sextant concealed in the prayer wheel; the artificial horizon was made with mercury placed in the wooden bowl which every Tibetan carries. Other essential instruments were stored away in the secret drawer of a strong wooden box.

Thus supplied and well trained, these remarkable men set forth on their various missions, with courage, determination and almost unequalled patience in the face of many dangers. One of them counted every step he took for 2,500 miles, crossing many mountains; another, for 2,080 miles, and so the work progressed. They measured with the prismatic compass the angles of all objects passed, monasteries and forts as well as mountain peaks.

They were a great little band—the Himalayan hillmen, Gurkhas, Tibetans, Sikkimese and Bhutanese lamas, as well as the survey specialists and topographers drawn from the Indian army. It would take a book to record the exploits of them all.

One incident will serve to show the unfailing persistence of all these native explorers. Kinthup, or K.P., a Sikkimese trained in the Indian survey department, had been picked out by Captain Harman, a leading Indian frontier geographer, to travel to Tibet with a Chinese lama and make his way from Lhasa to the great bend of the Tsangpo. To ascertain definitely whether or not the Tsangpo flowed into the Indian Brahmaputra, K.P. was instructed to cast into the river at this point specially marked logs of light wood. Watchers in Assam were to be on the lookout for the logs.

The Chinese lama at the first opportunity treacherously sold K.P. into the service of a wealthy Tibetan. After two years of slavery K.P. finally worked his way back to the Tsangpo, prepared five hundred logs and threw them into the river about thirty-five miles from the Assam border. Two of these logs, easily identifiable, were found several years later cast ashore on the banks of the Brahmaputra-Lohit in Assam, practically settling the question that the Tsangpo flowed into Assam and was part of the great Brahmaputra—a fact that was later established beyond a doubt.

The precision maps resulting from these explorations could not be kept secret indefinitely and hardly endeared the British in India to the suspicious and sensitive Tibetan authorities. Trade communications and direct relations between Tibet and India had progressed no farther than Warren Hastings' unsuccessful efforts of a century before. But when Tibetans invaded Sikkim and occupied a fort and mountain eighteen miles within its frontiers, the British Raj decided that definite measures had to be taken. Lurking always in the background was the fact that the Tibetan and Indian border touched for nearly two thousand miles from Kashmir to Burma. What would happen if a powerful and hostile country got possession of Tibet?

The British demanded the withdrawal of the Tibetan invaders. When neither the Chinese or Tibetan Governments paid heed to the communications, troops were sent to drive them out. What was wanted was the recognition of a British protectorate over Sikkim, delimitations of the Tibet-Sikkim frontier and the promotion of Indo-Tibetan trade. In 1890 a treaty was signed with China recognizing the British protectorate over Sikkim and defining the water divide of the Tista River as the boundary between Sikkim and Tibet. A trade treaty followed, establishing a trade mart for India at Yatung. The Tibetans refused to recognize the treaties on the ground that they had not signed them. At Yatung, an unsatisfactory place for a trade mart, the Tibetans built a wall across the narrow valley to prevent Indian and Tibetan traders from meeting. The boundary pillars on the Sikkim-Tibet frontier were destroyed. Lord Curzon, then Viceroy of India, tried to communicate directly with Tibet. His letters to the Dalai Lama were returned unopened.

The situation approached a crisis when the British learned that the Dalai Lama had sent an envoy extraordinary to Russia. The envoy extraordinary and his Tibetan suite were received cordially by the Czar and his ministers. It came about this way. Dorjieff, a Buriat Mongol, was a high lama and, as one of the tutors of the thirteenth Dalai Lama in his youth, had considerable influence over him. Born in Russian Siberia, Dorjieff was also a subject of the

Czar. He had frequently made trips to Russia to beg funds for his Tibetan monastery. He gave the Dalai Lama the impression not only that the friendship of the great Northern power would be worth having, but that more and more of the Czar's subjects were becoming Buddhists. Even the Czar himself was interested and likely to be converted! Envoy Extraordinary Dorjieff returned with many presents from the Czar to the Dalai Lama, including some Russian arms and ammunition and a handsomely brocaded set of Russian Church robes. To add to British anxiety, lively rumours were circulated that Russia and Tibet had signed a secret agreement. Russia vehemently and officially denied any agreement with or designs on Tibet.

All the same, the British decided that the time had come for action. Lord Curzon sent a mission, headed by Colonel Francis (later Sir Francis) Younghusband with a military escort of two hundred men to meet the Chinese Amban and Tibetan officials at Kampa Dzong, a small settlement a few miles across the Tibetan frontier from Sikkim, to discuss the whole problem of British-Indian relations with Tibet. Younghusband, with his staff of experts and his army escort, waited at Kampa Dzong from July to November, 1903, without achieving anything. All the Tibetans would say was, "Go back to Sikkim." They refused to negotiate. The British home government then sanctioned an advance. About twenty-five hundred British and Indian troops under the command of Brigadier General Macdonald took possession of the Chumbi Valley, and the Younghusband Mission, protected by some of these troops, started for Gyantse. Yatung was passed without trouble, and Phari, also, with troop reinforcements from Macdonald. They crossed the Tang-La in bitter, piercing January weather and set up their tents on the other side of the pass at the little village of Tuna, fifteen thousand feet above sea level.

For two months Younghusband tried again to negotiate, but the Tibetans refused to budge an inch and the monks with them were hostile and threatening. Toward the end of March, Macdonald moved up with about seven companies, two 10-pound guns and one 7-pounder. Younghusband announced to the Tibetans that he would move on to Gyantse on March 31 and warned them against obstructing the advance. As the expedition marched across the plain they sighted the Tibetans behind a series of breastworks on a ridge near Guru. Younghusband held one more futile parley with the Tibetans. If in fifteen minutes they did not leave their positions blocking the line of advance, Younghusband told them, they would be removed by force.

General Macdonald had only one hundred Englishmen and twelve hundred Indians, but they obeyed his command not to fire as they advanced up the hill against the fortified position of a Tibetan army of several thousand. Apparently the Tibetan troops did not want to fire either. The British-Indian forces crept around the flanks and were actually persuading the Tibetan soldiers to move away peacefully. Suddenly the Tibetan general, who was in the midst of the Indian sepoys, drew his revolver and shot a sepoy. This was the signal for battle. The Tibetan general was immediately killed. Later it was said that the General was egged on by a fanatical lama from Lhasa. Macdonald's troops had the best position and the best guns. But the Tibetans fought bravely with their old flintlocks and knives. After the action Macdonald's medical staff took care of the wounded Tibetans, but many had been killed. As Younghusband said, "It was a terrible and ghastly business."

The Younghusband Expedition marched on to Gyantse. Younghusband once more tried to negotiate with the Tibetans, and again all efforts to come to any terms were hopeless. There was more fighting at Gyantse, and

Macdonald, with stronger reinforcements, had to storm the great dzong, or fort, a formidable but successful operation.

It was now a year since Younghusband had arrived at Kampa Dzong. There was to be no more waiting. The Younghusband Expedition, supported by troops, set out for Lhasa, arriving on August 3, 1904. The Dalai Lama had fled to Urga, home of the third most important living god, and had appointed as regent and left his seals of office with the Ti Rimpoche, a highly respected old lama who was the chief doctor of divinity and metaphysics of Tibet.

With the assistance of the Chinese Resident, the Nepalese Representative and the Tongsa Penlop, later Maharaja of Bhutan, a treaty was signed between Great Britain and Tibet on September 7, 1904. Younghusband, with an eye to restoring British prestige in Tibet, insisted that it should be signed in the Potala. With Tibetans, Chinese, Bhutanese, British and Indian officers lining the great audience chamber and the Regent, the Chinese Resident and Younghusband seated at the latter's camp table, covered with the Viceroy of India's flag, and the five copies of the treaty brought in on a large silver tray, the ceremony of signing and affixing seals was a colourful and impressive occasion.

In signing this treaty Tibet agreed, among other things, to recognize the frontier between Sikkim and Tibet, as specified in the earlier treaty with China; to open trade marts to which British and Tibetan subjects were to have free access at Yatung, Gyantse and Gartok in western Tibet; to pay an indemnity for the attacks on the British mission and the expenses incurred in the dispatch of armed troops to Lhasa, and accept British occupation of the Chumbi Valley as security for the payment.

Especially important was the provision that without the consent of the British Government no portion of Tibetan territory should be ceded or otherwise given for occupation to any foreign power; no foreign power should be permitted to intervene in Tibetan affairs; no representative of any foreign power should be admitted to Tibet. Considering the indemnity terms too hard on Tibet, the British reduced them drastically and remained only three years in the Chumbi Valley. Nor did they stay in Lhasa. Younghusband was congratulated by the Viceroy, knighted by the British King-Emperor and grilled in the House of Commons for what was labelled "a massacre." Over the years he wrote many books on the East, dying in 1942 at the age of seventy-nine.

The Chinese Government, disturbed by the treaty, were anxious to restore their weakened power in Tibet. In 1906 they arranged a new treaty in Peiping with Great Britain, by which the latter agreed that Tibet's integrity should rest with China and that China and no other power should have the right to concessions in Tibet. This, in effect, delivered Tibet into the power of China, and China was not slow to take advantage of its opportunity. The British position was weakened and the treaty signed with Tibet in 1904 was little heeded.

After humiliating experiences in Peiping, the Dalai Lama returned to Lhasa at the end of 1909. The Chinese had seized much of eastern Tibet, desecrating monasteries and massacring Tibetans. On February 12, 1910, Chinese troops arrived in Lhasa, firing on the people. The following night the Dalai Lama fled with his ministers and a handful of soldiers, making a double-quick journey across the Sikkim frontier and on to Darjeeling.

During his stay in India the Dalai Lama was treated with all the courtesy and honour due to his rank. He never forgot the hospitality accorded him during his two years' exile in India. During his stay there he acquired a different idea of the British than he had when he fled from the Younghusband Expedition. In fact, he appealed to the British Government for assistance against Chinese aggression and would have liked to come under British protection. But that was not in accordance with British policy.

The Tibetans, roused to the boiling point against the Chinese, revolted in large numbers and succeeded in clearing them out of Central Tibet; the Dalai Lama returned to Tibet in June, 1912. By then the Chinese were concerned with their own internal problems and later fully occupied in the war with Japan. They had scarcely any extra strength to enforce what they considered, and the Tibetans denied, China's former suzerainty over Tibet. They never, however, relinquished their possession of the East Tibetan regions bordering on China's western frontier —regions which have always been historically, geographically and ethnically an integral part of Tibet.

As for the British, their position was strengthened after the return of the thirteenth Dalai Lama to his capital, but they did not interfere in Tibetan internal affairs. They posted their most tactful and friendly officials at the trade marts, many of them men with great knowledge of Tibetan life and customs and with real warmth for the Tibetan people. And Britain's "hands off" policy to other powers suited Tibet perfectly.

Since India achieved its independence in 1947, the British in India's diplomatic and civil service have been replaced one after the other by Indians. Hugh Richardson, the competent and popular head of the Indian mission in Lhasa, was the last Briton in India's Foreign Service. This tall, dark-haired Scotsman was most helpful to us. He answered many of our perplexing questions about Tibet. His first contact with that country was thirteen years ago when he was appointed British political officer at Gangtok. Through his long, close association with the Dalai Lama's government, Richardson probably knows more about present-day Tibet than any outsider. During the past decade he has spent as much time in Lhasa as he has at his Gangtok headquarters in Sikkim.

But Richardson had no intention of remaining permanently behind the Himalayas. In fact, in August, 1950, he relinquished his post as political officer and trade agent to Dr. S. Sinha of the External Affairs Ministry at Delhi. Hugh Richardson may soon come to America for a tour of lecturing followed by a professorship at one of our leading universities.

"Much of my service has been in Tibet," says Richardson, "and I shall be very sad to leave Lhasa. The Tibetans are a charming, friendly people. The country has a compelling attraction and there is a great store of interest in Tibetan religion, history, customs and wild life."

When Hugh Richardson learned of my intention to write this book he expressed the hope that it "will strengthen in many minds the belief not only that Tibet has a right to live its own life, but also that the peace and spiritual heritage of Tibet are qualities worth preserving in this contrary world."

India's present policy, as recently reported, is to interfere in no way with Tibetan affairs or with the relations of Tibet and China.

8

HALFWAY TO LHASA

LIKE Younghusband, but with an entirely different purpose, we set out from Phari for Gyantse, about another hundred miles. For several wearisome days our caravan paralleled one of the main stems of the Himalayas. Through the clouds we caught an occasional glimpse of sacred Chomolhari—"Goddess of the Mountains"—rising twenty-four thousand feet in all its majesty. Fresh snow had fallen on its rocky ridges and several huge, broken glaciers curled down from its summit. Most of the other peaks, all over twenty thousand feet, were hidden, except for the lower ends of countless huge tongues of ice, evidence of the mass of snow and ice above.

The Tibetan plateau that we were crossing is dreaded for its high winds that blow in all directions. Even in the summer, when we were travelling, they often reach gale force by afternoon. During the winter the wind and cold sweeping down from the Himalayan peaks are so intense on that fourteen-thousand-foot plain that the people are burned black; and they only go out when they must. It is a region of vast silent valleys that look like stretches of Wyoming, Utah and Nevada, if you can imagine those states raised to three, four and five times their present altitudes. Almost nothing grows at that height. The lakes we passed seemed silent and unreal.

Once in a while we rode by peasants ploughing their rocky fields with primitive, iron-tipped shares of wood drawn by the ubiquitous yak. We stopped to take pictures

G

97

of six teams ploughing together in one field. When our interpreter asked one farmer why they were ploughing zigzag from one corner of the field to the other, he explained that they did it to trap the demon that is in every field. Finally pushing him into a corner, they could then plough him right out of the field, thus ensuring a good crop.

At the base of Chomolhari we crossed the fifteen-thousand-foot Tang-La, second of the high passes on the road to Lhasa. Younghusband's Expedition came over this pass. The villages looked pretty much alike. All had the familiar thick-walled stone and mud-brick buildings, with prayer flags flapping from the roof tops in the stiff wind. Those days of double marches from Phari to Gyantse were tough ones—twenty-five and thirty miles at a stretch, sometimes on mules and sometimes on tiny, stiff-legged ponies. We, rather than the steeds, seemed to develop the saddle sores. Oh, our aching bottoms!

At the end of the first day we came to the windy town of Tuna, where Younghusband camped for two months. The next day brought us to Kala on the shores of a lake by that name; the third day, to Khangma; and the fourth, to Saugang.

The morning we left the little village of Saugang and its dak bungalow pleasantly shaded by willows, we rode through the gorges of the Nyang Chu, another tributary of the Tsangpo, as the Tibetans call the Brahmaputra. Coming out into a wide fertile valley, we caught sight of a distant fort, solitary and forbidding on the summit of a rock rising above the plain. This we knew was the famous Gyantse Dzong and, clustered below, was Gyantse, the third city of Tibet, although it was still too far away to see. Half a mile before we reached the fort, we crossed the river by a bridge hung with prayer flags that streamed in the breeze.

Gyantse, a focal centre for caravans to and from India, Nepal, Bhutan and Ladakh, as well as for internal travel in Tibet, is a lively trading centre. The white, flat-roofed houses stretch over a ridge, bending around somewhat in the shape of a crescent. Gyantse is completely dominated by the dzong and the large monastery at its foot near the market. Gyantse's market is rich in colour, human interest and activity. The goods are spread out on the ground or on rough tables and the merchants often sit under large umbrellas or awnings, where they enjoy gossiping as much as making sales. Here one finds Chinese brick tea, Tibetan salt and soda, dried fruits, jewellery, dyes, handwoven Tibetan rugs and bowls made of silver birch transported from Bhutan.

Wherever one goes in Gyantse, the dzong towers formidably over the scene. With its massive walls and commanding position it must have been invulnerable in the days when Chinese and Tibetans fought each other with medieval weapons. Even Younghusband's military escort had a tough job to make a breach in the wall with their ten-pound guns and storm the precipitous rock. Looking down through the narrow loopholes of the fort, one can understand how confident the Tibetans felt that their position was impregnable and how easily they expected to overwhelm the small British army below them. That was almost fifty years ago. Today in the era of atomic bombs, aeroplanes, tanks and bazookas, the dzong is only a museum piece.

Shortly after our caravan unloaded at the dak bungalow, a messenger came with word that we were about to have a visit from one of the top officials of Gyantse, a monk in a layman's job. This is not uncommon, since many monks combine high positions in religious and temporal affairs.

An hour later he came—Khenchung Lama. A remarkable and striking figure, the Lama. In a golden silk gown

99

brocaded with dragons, a two-storey golden hat shaped a little like a lampshade, and adorned with elaborate turquoise and gold jewellery, he looked, I imagine, as Genghis or Kublai Khan may have looked. His little fingernail was an inch long, as in the oldtime fashion of the upper-class Chinese, and he had a long pigtail, of course. The Lama presented us with the unfailing white scarves, and his servants gave us a bag of grain for our animals and a tray piled high with a hundred eggs—both fresh and ancient.

After the usual polite exchange of formalities, we launched into a discussion of Tibetan ideas, too difficult to handle smoothly through the medium of an interpreter, who leaned more to the concrete than the abstract. The Lama seemed deeply religious, a man of culture and learning in his own Tibetan-Buddhist field. And eloquent, too, as I realized from his long, easy flow of Tibetan, which was Greek to me until translated into a few short sentences, tantalizing because they conveyed only the barest idea of what he was saying. He wanted me to know Tibetan leaders devote nearly all their time to spiritual thought and meditation.

"But how about the other four million everyday Tibetans?" I inquired.

He pondered over that a few moments and explained with some firmness: "*All* Tibetans concentrate on thoughts of Buddha, Nirvana and their next incarnation. Therefore, any imports from the West—ideas, science or inventions—are superficial and trivial and have no importance for us."

Tsewong, our interpreter, a graduate of one of India's best agricultural colleges, said, "The Lama's comments are too deep for me." We left it at that.

During our short stay in Gyantse we visited the large monastery adjoining the market at the foot of the dzong. In the great prayer hall, dimly lighted, a thousand monks were chanting their service before a gilded Buddha, fifty feet high. We drank yak-butter tea in an upper room with some of the older monks and walked for a half-mile or so around the monastery roofs and balconies. Marvelling, we watched a pilgrim prostrate himself before a Buddhist image, rise in attitude of prayer, and fall forward again on his face. He had been keeping up this performance for a week, and intended to continue his routine without interruption for a month—every day from dawn to dusk.

Two well-known travellers, I recalled, spent some time in Gyantse and wrote vivid accounts of this same monastery. One was William Montgomery McGovern, who went to Lhasa in disguise, and the other, Theos Bernard, officially invited and the third American to visit Lhasa.

For many years now Dr. McGovern has been professor of political science at Northwestern University. In his youth he lived in Japan, delved seriously into Mahayana Buddhism and even received an honorary Buddhist ordination from the Great Buddhist temple in Kyoto. Brilliant and precocious, he was at twenty-two on the faculty of London University's School of Oriental Studies. Because of his theoretical knowledge of the Tibetan language and customs, he was invited to join an expedition of four specialists setting out for Tibet to make a scientific survey of the country and its people. This was in 1922. The India Office in London and the government of India allowed the party to travel to Gyantse, where they could apply to the Tibetan government for permission to proceed to Lhasa and other parts of the interior. They crossed into Tibet over the Nathu Pass and followed the same route we took to Gyantse; only they travelled slowly in order to make observations along the way.

David Macdonald, whose mother was a Sikkimese, was the British trade agent at Gyantse then. He hospitably received the group and forwarded their petition to Lhasa. For two or three weeks they busied themselves in and around Gyantse, ingratiating themselves with local officials and high lamas, while they waited anxiously for favourable word from Lhasa. The word finally came, and it was a decisive no. Thinking there still might be a chance if the party was reduced, three of the men returned to India. Captain J. E. Ellam, co-leader of the expedition, and McGovern remained in Gyantse to send another petition to the Lhasa authorities. If not to Lhasa, could they go to Shigatse? If not to Shigatse, could they stay a few months longer in Gyantse to continue their researches? The answer came back in no uncertain terms. They were to leave Tibet immediately.

McGovern was bitterly disappointed. He wanted to attempt the trip by himself at once "in secret and in disguise." But he remembered a promise he had given to the British political officer in Gangtok that he would return to India in case of refusal, and decided to return to Darjeeling with Ellam. Once back in Darjeeling he felt that he was free from his spoken promise. And so he "began making active steps for a new undertaking, for I was determined that come what might I should make one more attempt to reach the sacred city of the Buddhas, if necessary even by stealth and by disguise."

McGovern took a month for his preparations, making a secret visit to Kalimpong to purchase three mules and three ponies and hiring four servants, all Sikkimese, in Darjeeling. The first, a native secretary, was dubbed Satan and well deserved the name from the way he treated McGovern, who had to play the role of servant in Tibet. Lhaten, the bearer, who had been with McGovern on the first trip to Gyantse, joined up again. The others were a *syce*, or groom to take care of the animals, and a half-witted boy to serve as an odd man. Since it was impossible to depart "secretly" from Darjeeling, one of the most gossipy towns in the world, McGovern let the word out that he was making a two-months' tour of Sikkim, climbing some of the mountains to do geological work.

It was January 10, 1923, when the little party set out from Darjeeling—a terrible time of year to cross the snow-blocked passes. McGovern had to avoid his former route through Sikkim and along the Tibetan trail from the Chumbi Valley to Gyantse, where he was already known and would be recognized. After all kinds of difficulties, misery and illness, tracking over unfamiliar Sikkim mountains in snow, ice and blizzards, and stopping when they could in dirty, deserted little huts, he and his men finally dropped down into Tibet without discovery and reached the little settlement of Kampa Dzong, where Younghusband in 1903 had waited in vain for five months to make a treaty with Tibet.

Just before crossing the frontier, McGovern put on his disguise. His blonde hair was dyed. Stripping to the skin in a bitter early morning wind, he had Lhaten daub his whole body with a special mixture of walnut juice and iodine. McGovern's blue eyes were a genuine problem. He squeezed the juice of a lemon into them. It was painful, but was supposed to give the eyes a darker shade. As an extra precaution he daubed glue under his lids to imitate the secretions due to snow blindness, and for a final touch he put on dark goggles. He hid his European clothes under a rock and put on one of the three Tibetan coolie costumes he had brought with him. This too was the moment for Satan to deck himself out in a fine robe— the kind worn by a Sikkimese noble. From that moment Satan was the master and McGovern was the servant. Nor was McGovern given much chance to forget his subordinate position.

North from Kampa Dzong, he took a little-travelled route considerably west of the more popular road to Gyantse, which he naturally avoided. The little caravan even went through Shigatse and then turned east for Lhasa on a short-cut used by the postal couriers, but rarely by pilgrims and caravans. McGovern's feet were blistered and bleeding, the coarse food disagreed with him, he had dysentery, and the wind bit through his thin coolie garments. He craved unobtainable sugar as an alcoholic craves his bottle and, to top everything, he slipped through thin river ice into equally icy water and injured his hip. He was strongly tempted to abandon the effort to reach Lhasa but, remembering all the trials and tribulations already endured, he grimly set his teeth and went on.

From Tibetans he met, he learned that rumours were abroad that one McGovern was probably in Tibet on his way to Lhasa and that local officials had been ordered to keep a sharp lookout for a foreigner. But when he came to the point where the side road joined the main highway leading from Gyantse to Lhasa, there was no choice. He had to take it. By amazing luck he got through with his companions straight into Lhasa, on February 16, 1923, on the last day of the Tibetan year, just as the three weeks of New Year festivities were to begin. Lhasa was more jammed than an American city during a Legion convention, but his faithful Lhaten begged a lodging for the night, saying that they were a small party of devout Sikkimese pilgrims. Exhausted, McGovern was dumped in a tiny out-room. When the little dog belonging to the family started barking ceaselessly, probably sniffing an alien, McGovern decided to give himself up.

Barging into the inner rooms, he found the head of the household. It was Sonam, the Tibetan official in charge of the new communication system between India and Tibet. It was Sonam who had given the orders to make a special search for McGovern. Naturally they both were startled at this unexpected and dramatic meeting. But Sonam behaved handsomely. He arranged a midnight supper, gave McGovern his own comfortable room and planned to inform the Dalai Lama privately the next day of McGovern's arrival. McGovern had to appear before the officials, but he was treated very well.

Since it was the custom for two monks from Drepung monastery to take over the administration of Lhasa during the three weeks of New Year celebrations, when throngs of fanatical monks and pilgrims come to Lhasa, it was thought advisable for McGovern to remain quietly at Sonam's residence, without venturing into the streets. But he was hardly a prisoner. In his book *To Lhasa in Disguise*, he describes a mob gathering in the street outside the place where he was staying, throwing stones and sticks and shouting "Death to the foreigner." As soon as the New Year festival was over and the crowds of monks had departed, he sallied forth on a number of excursions, and on March 24 he was given papers, fresh transport animals, permits for the rest-houses and an armed escort to the Indian frontier.

It seems a far cry from Arizona to Tibet, but it was not too far for Theos Bernard. One might have expected Bernard, who was born in Arizona, to have the outlook of a native of one of America's most picturesque western states. But from his parents, who had long followed the religious and philosophical teachings of Asia, he acquired his own interest in Eastern philosophy and spent several years studying in India and Sikkim, with special emphasis on Buddhist teachings.

In 1937 he decided to visit Tibet. Like McGovern he received permission to go to Gyantse and have his petition to enter Lhasa forwarded to the authorities. At that time the thirteenth Dalai Lama had been dead several years and the new incarnate Dalai Lama had not yet been found. Bernard stayed several weeks in Gyantse, combining his interest in monasteries and lamaism with some of the gay parties that the British organized in those days when they headed the Gyantse trade mission. The Tibetans were given to understand that Bernard was profoundly interested in learning more about their religion and that he himself was a devotee of yoga practices. After a few weeks Bernard received his answer—an invitation from the ruling regent and from the Kashag, the high governing body of Lhasa, to visit the capital. Naturally he was in high spirits —who wouldn't have been? Bernard was warmly received by Tibetan officials, entertained royally and given handsome presents on his departure. He had visited many monasteries and taken many photographs. On his return to America he went on a number of lecture tours, showing his pictures, and he also gave lessons in yoga.

Bernard undoubtedly had a yearning to return to Tibet. Since he did not have a second invitation, he must have planned to enter secretly. Early in November, 1947, dispatches from New Delhi reported that Bernard and his servants had been killed by tribal raiders in the Himalayas. But on November 17 the papers announced that Bernard's American publisher had received a letter from Mrs. Bernard dated November 5 from Calcutta, stating that although tribesmen had killed the carriers, her husband was safe. His present whereabouts was unknown, she said. That was the last word received in this country about the fate of Theos Bernard. Was he alive? Did he disappear into one of those Tibetan monasteries, which he described, where holy men shut themselves in cavelike grottoes for the rest of their lives? It all seemed quite a mystery—a theme for a movie thriller.

When we were in Lhasa we inquired about him of some of our Tibetan friends. All of them agreed that Bernard had been killed. The bodies of his servants were found. Although his body was never found, they said he had unquestionably been murdered too. The Tibetans told us that they were amazed and puzzled at the way Bernard kept changing his costume when he was in Lhasa. One day he would wear a Tibetan nobleman's outfit and the next day he would appear in the robes worn by the abbot of a monastery. But what puzzled them most was that when he returned to America he called himself "a white lama."

9

IN TIBETAN HOMES

AT Gyantse we were about halfway to the capital. Here the trade route from India branches off. The main highway continues north-east to Lhasa, and another road turns north-west to Shigatse, Tibet's second city and the seat of the Tashi Lhunpo, the Panchen Lama's great monastery. A side trip to Shigatse was a temptation, but the days were slipping by fast. We were eager to forge ahead to have as much time as possible in the holy city of lamaism.

Gyantse also marks the end of the line as far as Indian and western influence is concerned. Here the Indian mail service terminates, and very few travellers, except religious pilgrims and Asian traders, are permitted to go farther into Tibet. From Gyantse to Lhasa there would be no more of those comfortable dak bungalows that had looked so good to us at the end of each day's trek. Now our overnight stops would be made in the homes of Tibetan villagers. After we left Gyantse we began to enjoy the sensation of being actually in the heart of the world's most remote and secluded country.

Any introduction to a Tibetan house is an unforgettable experience. Ours came at the end of the first day's march from Gyantse—at the village of Gobshi. Here we were taken to a two-storey stone dwelling. As in most homes in Tibet that are not yak-hair tents, the ground floor was reserved for caravan animals, plus the owner's yaks, cows, goats and chickens. The usual vicious, snarling mastiff that guards a Tibetan household lunged at us from the end of a yak rope in the courtyard.

To reach the living quarters we mounted a rickety ladder which landed us in an upper patio, with dirt-floored rooms on all sides. One was a smoke-filled kitchen with a hole in the roof for a chimney; another, a dark, cell-like compartment with Tibetan Buddhist images surrounded by metal dishes, holding the yak-butter lamps that are lighted during devotions. The living quarters were devoid of furniture, except for two low divans and a low red-lacquered table in each cubicle. The plumbing? It was of the outdoor variety—a slit in the floor over the manure pile downstairs. It all seemed grim indeed. But it provided shelter from the fierce night winds.

Norbu, our cook, immediately made himself at home in the primitive kitchen and prepared supper over two fires of yak dung, with the assistance of our Colman fox-hole primus stove that operated on kerosene. Tibetan eyes bulged whenever Norbu used that primus; its intense flame seemed to them like some kind of magic. What really was a miracle to me was the fine meal that he concocted in that unlighted, smoke-filled kitchen. He really was an expert chef for an expedition like ours and, besides, he knew all the tricks of Tibetan cooking. Along the kitchen walls the fuel was piled—cakes of dung. A young girl was churning butter in a hollow cylindrical wooden tube, about four feet high—singing as she worked the plunger up and down.

Our Gobshi hosts implored us to use their largest and most elegant room, occupying one side of the patio. Like the other rooms, it had a dirt floor, but several tapestries adorned the walls, and the divans at opposite ends of the room were covered with Tibetan rugs. We thanked our hosts and declined the honour, preferring to pitch our tent on the roof and sleep on our own army cots.

Next morning we were up at the crack of dawn with the household rooster. We washed in a copper pan and brushed our teeth out of cups, spitting over the edge of the roof. To take care of our other important needs we had to hike out among the rocks. After a breakfast of porridge and eggs, we mounted our ponies and headed on up the gorge for the eighteen miles to Ralung.

According to his own words put down on the trip, my father enjoyed the meals on the road to Lhasa with as much relish as the most delectable repast prepared by America's exacting Gourmet Society, if not more. He was, after all, taking his first vacation in many years, and he has a way of extracting the utmost pleasure from his experiences. I must admit that Dad is a better scout than I am. Even though we travelled luxuriously indeed compared to the privations endured by some of the European pioneers who ventured into a very forbidden Tibet, I still insist that our diet was a bit monotonous. I don't want to see another prune or dried apple for years.

I quote straight from my father's diary to give you some idea of his reaction to the meals served on the journey to Lhasa:

"We are sitting in a Tibetan kitchen with ten other people. In one corner two women are trying to start a yak-dung fire in a stove made of stone and mud. One of the women is vigorously pushing up and down on a goat-skin, a primitive Tibetan bellows. Six others are watching Tsewong Norbu, as he putters with Lowell Jr.'s stove.

"The spectators, looking like brigands in a Robin Hood opera, squat around me, drinking the omnipresent Tibetan tea, which is mixed with barley and rancid yak butter. One old crone and a patriarch are goggle-eyed as the pressure cooker gets going. They can't understand where that intense flame comes from. No doubt they think the Buddha works miracles through strange people.

IN TIBETAN HOMES

"Three more persons have come in. I can hardly make them out through the smoke. Having no chimneys, only holes in the roof, Tibetan kitchens are black and suffocating. They are always on the second floor because the animals, the chickens and the mud are in full possession of the first floor.

"Thanks to tips from Suydam Cutting and to Lowell Jr.'s past experience preparing food in Alaska, with the Dartmouth Outing Club on Mount Washington, and during his recent travels in the back country of Turkey and Persia, we are doing all right on this journey to Lhasa, as far as meals are concerned. Food is the one department in which we shine, and ours is international, too. It has been brought together from practically everywhere.

"Take breakfast. We start with stewed apple rings from India, or prunes from Australia, or sliced fresh peaches from nearby Bhutan. Next, cream of wheat—labelled in many languages and made I don't know where—or porridge of Tibetan barley, or our own American Quaker Oats. Then, bread baked on the trail, of Australian self-raising flour; Australian tinned butter specially packed for the tropics; something mysterious, labelled bacon, from Australia; and Tibetan eggs. Our breakfast drink, tea from India.

"Lunch we always eat on the march, sitting on a pile of rocks, beside one of the tributaries of the Brahmaputra, with peaks from 19,000 to 21,000 feet high circling all around us. Lunch usually consists of water biscuits from England, sardines from Norway, cheese from Switzerland, a block of unsweetened chocolate from England, dates from Persia, and Tibetan snow water, highly chlorinated in case a herd of yak might have been grazing nearby.

"Seated on Tibetan rugs around a charcoal brazier, by the light of a primitive oil lamp, we usually have quite a feast for dinner. How's this for a menu?

"A spot of Canadian Club, from General Willoughby, MacArthur's second in command in Tokyo. Then pea soup from Switzerland, concentrated in a block an inch square. Next, ragout de veau with gravy from Switzerland or Tibetan mutton—the gift of a Dzong-pön (a district governor)—stewed together with fresh turnips, cauliflower, beets and carrots, all local products. Usually we have a plate of rice from the sack presented to us by another Tibetan official. We top off our banquet with pancakes made with Australian flour and strawberry jam from Tasmania, and Klim, our powdered milk from America.

"It all tastes wonderful, due to the wizardry of cook Tsewong Norbu, who, to our good fortune, served an Englishman for seven years in India and Afghanistan."

The first two marches out of Gyantse took us winding upward through a deep gorge. All around us were barren mountains. No trees or flowers grew at this high altitude. But these bleak slopes were obviously rich in iron and other valuable ores. The rock walls were streaked with veins and the rocks along the trail and under the ponies' hooves looked promising. We were positive that there were quantities of gold in those mountains. We noticed a great abundance of quartz in which several types of minerals were embedded, but sharply as we looked we could not find any gold nuggets. I was sorry that we could not stop long enough to try panning for stray bits of gold among the sand and pebbles in some of the mountain streams we passed.

From time immemorial Tibetans have washed gold from their streams. Early travellers and later travellers, such as Rockhill and Hedin, have commented on the crude, superficial workings of gold fields in western, northern and eastern Tibet. Unquestionably the Tibetan Himalayas are an unexplored and virgin source of tremendous mineral wealth, not only gold, but iron, copper, lead, mercury and most likely uranium, too. If the Tibetans would be willing to exploit their mineral deposits, the prosperity and living standards of the country could be greatly increased. But there is a strong feeling against any effective shaft mining for fear of arousing the anger and revenge of the spirits that dwell under the earth.

Rockhill, back in 1891, gave an interesting explanation of the prejudice against digging into the earth: "Mining is not allowed in Tibet, as there exists a deep-rooted superstition, carefully fostered by the lamas, that if nuggets of gold are removed from the earth no more gold will be found in the river gravels, the nuggets being the roots or plants whereof the gold dust is the grains or flowers." The superstitions still hold and probably are encouraged by the Tibetan ruling class on the basis that in the process of developing a mining industry Tibet itself might be exploited and swallowed up by more powerful neighbouring countries.

We met with the same simple and friendly peasant hospitality in Ralung as in Gobshi, and spent the night in a house of mud and rock similar to our Gobshi shelter. Our animals slept downstairs in a slush of mud; we were taken upstairs, where it was considerably drier. Ralung was even smaller and dingier than Gobshi. From snow peaks a few miles away, a muddy torrent of water rushed past our house. The high point of our stay was Norbu's special treat, a batch of pancakes, made from Australian self-raising flour, served piping hot with butter and strawberry jam. Norbu continued to amaze us with his culinary talent.

Again we tried our tent on the roof, but not so successfully as in Gobshi. We almost blew away during the night; the tent flapped wildly, its guy-ropes snapping against the canvas sides. As if our tent problems were not enough, a group of monks, deciding it was an auspicious night to drive the demons from a nearby hut, beat on drums and blasted their horns of bone without pause. It hardly sounded like music to us, just a terrific racket. We had no sleep that night, but the demon must have been frightened away.

The monastery at Ralung is unusual. We were told that in this lamasery monks and nuns live together under the same roof. They belong to a sect which permits marriage. It was one big happy family, with many children—all the boys to become monks and the girls destined to be nuns like their parents. Ralung went even a step beyond what we encountered at Gyantse. On the slope above the town are four Buddhist religious retreats: two for monks, two for nuns. In one monastery and one nunnery celibacy is strictly observed. In the other two the discipline is not so demanding and, as a result, many babies are dedicated to the service of Buddha. But Ralung and Gyantse are exceptions. The majority of Tibetan lamaseries impose vows of celibacy on their members.

On our seventeenth day out of Gangtok, capital of Sikkim, we started from Ralung on our longest day's march—thirty-two miles. In a car at home that distance would take about forty-five minutes. But thirty-two miles across Tibet on the road to Lhasa is another matter. It took our caravan fourteen hours.

On the first eight miles from Ralung we rode rapidly down a wide, lonely valley—not a sign of life except an occasional caravan. Then we began to climb through a gorge between cliffs—rich in iron and other minerals. For hours in a pouring rain we mounted steadily toward the Karo-La, between giant mountains from which glaciers sent their waters cascading towards one of the many tributaries of the Brahmaputra. Near the summit of the Karo-La, a 16,600-foot pass, we were squeezed in between three great glaciers, walls of ice only a few yards from our stony trail.

After scaling the Karo-La, we collided on the other side with the longest caravan of yaks we had met on our whole journey. Either our string of pack animals or the yaks had to give way. The trail was not wide enough for both. So the Chogpon, our military escort, drove those hundreds of yaks over the edge with his whip and at a precipitous place, too. But the yak is an incredible animal. In spite of his size he can cling to a mountain wall with his cloven hooves where no horse or mule would venture. A little farther on we had to detour around a place where an avalanche of snow from a mountain peak had completely wiped out our trail.

Just over the pass we stopped at an inn frequented by yak herdsmen to dry ourselves out and have a comforting cup of tea. It was the dirtiest and smokiest hovel we had stumbled into—and we had seen plenty. Even the mule-teers objected to spending the night in that dump. Still rubbing our eyes from the smoke in the hut, we pushed off in the rain for another sixteen miles.

"You know," remarked Dad, as we rode along, "I believe the Suydam Cuttings stayed a night at that inn when they were in Tibet."

"Well, I don't envy them the experience," I said.

"I'm afraid those dak bungalows spoiled us and we're getting a little soft," Dad observed. "We're travelling very de luxe. Do you remember how Madame David-Neel made her way to Lhasa?"

Of course I remembered. She was the first western woman to reach the Forbidden City. She came there un-invited and in disguise, and she lived in Lhasa for two months without being discovered. That was in 1925.

No one ever set forth so well equipped to undertake a journey in disguise to Lhasa as this remarkable French-woman, Alexandra David-Neel. A student of Sanskrit and oriental philosophies and religions, she already knew something of Tibetan literature and the Tibetan language. In Burma, Nepal, China, Japan and Korea she had studied and meditated in famous monasteries. For a time she lived in Sikkim, and legally adopted as her son a young Tibetan boy who was later ordained as a lama and known as Yongden Lama. On one of her journeys to Tibet she succeeded in penetrating as far as Shigatse, where the Panchen Lama—the one who fled to China and died there in exile in 1937—showered her with attention when he recognized her zeal and interest in the study of lamaism. Although the Panchen Lama was eager to help Madame David-Neel in her researches in every way and pressed her to make an extended stay, it was not long before the Lhasa authorities ordered her to leave the country. She had not been officially invited!

This enforced departure, combined with the fines poor villagers in the neighbourhood of Shigatse had to pay for not reporting her, rankled bitterly. She said: "I must confess that, unlike most travellers who have attempted to reach Lhasa and have failed to reach their goal, I never entertained a strong desire to visit the sacred lamaist city. As for my researches regarding the literature, philosophy and secret lore of Tibet, these things could be pursued more profitably among the literati and mystics in the freely accessible and more intellectual parts of north-eastern Tibet than in the capital. What decided me to go to Lhasa was, above all, the absurd prohibition which closes Tibet."

Madame David-Neel did not concern herself with politics, but she felt strongly that Tibet should not be closed to explorers, scientists, scholars and other "honest and well-meaning" travellers. It was her strong conviction that the British were wholly responsible for the situation. A few years after her Shigatse experience, she set out with her adopted son and one servant from Jakyendo, a market town on the Lhasa road, with the intention of making an eighteen-months' journey through Tibet. As she was nearing the Salween River, she was stopped and again was ordered out of the country. This time she was determined to take action.

"It was then," she wrote in her introduction to *My Journey to Lhasa*, "that the idea of visiting Lhasa really became implanted in my mind. Before the frontier post to which I had been escorted I took an oath that in spite of all obstacles I would reach Lhasa and show what the will of a woman could achieve! But I did not think only of avenging my own defeats. I wanted the right to exhort others to pull down the antiquated barriers which surround, in the centre of Asia, a vast area extending approximately from 79 to 99 degrees longitude."

As a professed Buddhist of the ascetic type, Madame David-Neel was always able to gain the confidence of scholarly lamas. Writing, understanding and speaking fluently many Tibetan dialects, she could in a good disguise pass at least for a pilgrim from one of the Buddhist regions bordering on Tibet. With her love of humour and lively interest in people, her courage and willingness to meet every obstacle, she was ready to set forth and "show what the will of a woman could achieve."

So on Madame David-Neel's fifth journey into Tibet, Lhasa was her definite goal. Starting out in the early autumn with Yongden through the frontier section, which was under Chinese rule, she went by way of Likiang, crossing the Salween River into the heart of Tibet. They took on the roles of poor religious pilgrims partly begging their way. Yongden, as a lama of the Red Hat sect, wore the robes of his order, but very shabby ones. Madame David-Neel, in even shabbier Tibetan dress, travelled as his aged mother. She dyed her brown hair with black Chinese ink, which often had to be renewed, and lengthened it by adding jet black yak's hair. As a finishing touch she powdered her face with a mixture of cocoa and crushed charcoal. Under their clothes they concealed money belts and revolvers to meet any emergency. They had no carriers with them. Alone and carrying heavy loads on their backs, they walked all the way to Lhasa.

For fear of detection they proceeded at first mostly by night and concealed themselves in caves or behind rocks during the daytime. They lived on a scanty diet of buttered tea and *tsamba*, but many times they went twenty-four hours and longer without any food. As the weather grew more severe and they had to scale the high snow passes, they often slept in the open on the snow with their little tent wrapped around them. They carried no blankets, and the tent usually served as their only protection against the bitter cold. They dared not put it up until they got farther into the country.

Realizing that they really passed as mendicant pilgrims with the Tibetans, they gained more confidence in their disguise, and no longer tried to detour around villages. Sometimes they begged for shelter in a peasant hut and sat and slept on rough kitchen floors filthy with grease from soup, butter and other muck. Sometimes Yongden bought food supplies at a monastery, leaving his "poor old mother" to wait outside. As a Red Hat, Yongden was often pressed to tell fortunes and indicate where a lost cow was or whether a law-suit would turn out successfully —all matters which he handled with great discretion. Madame David-Neel, tied to a hook, had to swing across rivers above high gorges on sagging leather cables; she and her adopted son were snow-blocked for several days on a high pass in a blizzard and almost starved before they worked their way down; they had a narrow escape from robbers. But always she kept her sense of humour and, ignoring the many risks and hardships, she viewed the whole experience as a glorious adventure and a rare opportunity to get close to the lives of the poor, everyday folk of Tibet. Her only fear was that she might be discovered before she reached Lhasa.

Disguised as pious beggars, they frequently had to solicit food and alms to avoid suspicion. But when they felt safe in the heart of Tibet, they purchased supplies, sometimes being "extravagant beggars," as Madame David-Neel expressed it, indulging in molasses cakes, dried fruits and plenty of butter. It was the most economical journey she had ever taken. During the four-months' walk from Yunnan to Lhasa the two of them succeeded in spending only one hundred rupees.

They slipped unnoticed into Lhasa with the great throngs arriving for the New Year festivals. Finding lodgings in a hovel occupied by poor beggars, they felt that their incognito was safe. After the long, hard journey on foot, Madame David-Neel was determined to reap her reward by attending all the festivals and viewing all the sights of the Holy City. And during a two-months' stay she visited everything from the Potala to the butter festival as one of the Tibetan tourist crowd. She was usually taken for a Ladakhi and, rather gloating over her talent as an actress, she even put on a show in the market place, bargaining for an aluminium saucepan at a ridiculous price, talking nonsense and making the more sophisticated Lhasa shoppers laugh at the peasant woman who came from the cattle and grass country. That act was really a triumph, because she pulled it when she saw a policeman eyeing her intently and suspiciously.

She left Lhasa as quietly as she had come, but she and Yongden set out in comfort as middle-class Tibetans on ponies, with carriers. It did not matter now if they were caught. Since they were on their way from, instead of to, Lhasa, no one paid much attention to them. At Gyantse she called on David Macdonald, the part-Tibetan British trade agent, and astonished him and his colleagues with a brief account of her adventures and her undiscovered visit to Lhasa. It was, Macdonald said, "a wonderful feat for a woman of her age and physique. She appeared very frail and, to succeed as she had, called for immense courage and vitality."

During the Second World War Madame David-Neel

spent several years on the Chinese-Tibetan frontier, often suffering real privation, cut off as she was from her funds in France. But she was a keen observer, and learned a great deal about China's far west and the intrigues of the border country. In 1946 she returned to France and to her home in the Basse-Alpes, where, at more than eighty years of age, she is still working quietly on her researches in Tibetan religion and literature. She won a victory for herself, but Tibet is still closed!

10

THE FINAL PUSH TO LHASA

CONTINUING our longest day's march, we came to one of the highest and most beautiful lakes in the world —Yamdrok Tso, the Turquoise Lake, or Lake of the Upland Pastures. This fresh-water lake is at an altitude of more than fourteen thousand feet and runs sixty miles through the Himalayas.

Approaching the village and lofty fort of Nagartse Dzong on the shore of the lake, we overtook a man who was loping along with a sack on his back and a spear in his hand. He was one of the Tibetan mail carriers. They travel on foot, running most of the way. The spear is the carrier's badge of office. After five or six miles another man seizes the mail bag. It is a day-and-night relay race against time between Lhasa and Gyantse, where the Indian Government takes over the postal service to India. As we rode up to his heels, he turned without stopping, stuck out his tongue in the Tibetan polite greeting and challenged us to a race, he on foot, carrying the mail, our party on horseback. It was a neck-and-neck race.

At Nagartse we inquired at once for the "Thunderbolt Sow." Colonel Ilia Tolstoy of the OSS had told about his visit to her during the war. The abbess of an all-male monastery on the hill above Yamdrok Tso, she is the holiest woman in Tibet. Regarded as an incarnation of Dorje Phamo, the Thunderbolt Sow, she is supposed to have the power to transform herself into a sow. The story goes that one of the early Thunderbolt Sows transformed not only herself but all the lamas in her monastery into pigs when an enemy army threatened the monastery. The invaders were so frightened that they fled. Anyway, that's the way the tale runs. Tibet teems with strange tales, and the story of the Thunderbolt Sow is one of the strangest. The Dorje Phamo is the only Tibetan woman permitted to ride in a palanquin; also the only one who is blessed by the hand of the Dalai Lama instead of being touched by the red tassel at the end of a short wand, as are all other women and commoners.

When Tolstoy visited Nagartse in 1942, the present incarnation was five years old. Now she is thirteen. We were eager to meet and film the little abbess, but her monastery, Samden Gompa, five or six miles from Nagartse, was difficult to reach because of the floods. So we had to be satisfied with the incredible and wondrous stories relayed to us about the Thunderbolt Sow and with predictions of the fate probably in store for the thirteen-year-old abbess. Tibet's Number One Oracle, we were informed, was about to look into the past and the future and pronounce whether she was the true Dorje Phamo or whether a nun in another part of Tibet was the genuine incarnation of the original sacred sow and should replace the present occupant.

Another day along the shores of the enchanting Yamdrok Tso brought us to the village of Pedi, where we spent the night. As we rode away from Pedi the next morning, the sun broke through for a few moments, and we noticed numerous gulls and bar-headed geese. Our caravan was about to ford a stream near the shore of the lake when we observed that the waters were black with a strange kind of trout, making their way upstream to spawn. Norbu, the cook, with his mind on the evening meal, waded into the stream and in a few minutes had scooped out with his bare hands sixteen beautiful fish, that ranged in length from ten to fourteen inches. The few towns around the lake might easily support themselves on the fish of Yamdrok Tso, but fishing in Tibet, like hunting and mining, is forbidden for religious reasons. According to Sir Charles Bell, fish, pork and some poultry and eggs are believed to contain "black pills," due to the wicked crimes—usually the destruction of many lives—committed by the animals in the previous incarnation. Tibetans avoid eating any food which contains these "black pills," convinced that such a sacrilege will bring down on them serious spiritual harm and misfortune.

Our third and final pass on the way to the Holy City was 16,200-foot Nyapso-La, which separates Yamdrok Tso from the Valley of the great Brahmaputra. Far up in the clouds at the summit of Nyapso, we paused to look back at this most enchanting of lakes. The sun broke through for a few moments, brilliantly intensifying the blue-green waters, set like a precious jewel in a glorious circle of mountains.

Passing a yak caravan near the prayer flags at the top of the pass, we saw the Brahmaputra far below through breaks in a bank of cloud wisps. The descending trail was so steep and so badly washed out that we dismounted to give our panting ponies a break. Scrambling over the slippery grass and rocks, we worked our way down to the Brahmaputra, winding and turning through the valley more than four thousand feet below.

Another night in a Tibetan hut in Singlakenjung, a town on the south bank of the Brahmaputra! Then we had the fun of riding in comfort down the river in skin boats. Our two coracles were made of yak-skin stretched taut over a framework of willow ribs. The Tibetans call these flat-bottomed boats *kowas*. They are about ten feet long, six feet wide at the blunt end and two feet wide at the other end, where the oarsmen sit. Our *kowas*, carrying us and our baggage with the greatest of ease, were lashed together at their blunt ends. Their sides were about three feet high and they were held together by tough yak-hide thongs. The oars were almost as unusual as the boats. To the end of a long pole, apparently of cedar, were lashed two flat pieces of wood to serve as a paddle. Each of these strange, light river boats can carry the loads of twenty pack animals—more than a ton of freight. In our coracles were squeezed eight persons in addition to the loads, and of course the two *kobos*, the leather-skinned boatmen. They sang a boat song, curious and haunting to our western ears, as they struggled to keep us in midstream. We made a recording of their singing on our portable machine. Later Dad was told that his description of the boat trip, combined with the *kobos'* singing, was one of his most popular broadcasts from Tibet.

We were now headed down the Brahmaputra for the sixteen miles to Chusul, to begin the final push to Lhasa. In our skin coracles we were rushing along at about ten miles per hour.

Just before coming into sight of Chusul we raced through a narrow gorge between high cliffs. On one was perched a monastery, and any number of Buddhas were painted on the rocks to pacify the river demons. The gorge was filled with prayer flags, some planted in regimental lines out into the river; doubtless to protect coracles from the evil spirits and to guide boatmen away from submerged rocks.

Rounding a rocky promontory, we were in Chusul, situated at the point where the Kyi Chu tears, raging, into the Brahmaputra. Our *kobos* had a strenuous job to pull us out of the clutches of the current, but, aided by lusty shouts and the rhythm of their boat song, they succeeded. The Tibetan boatmen cannot row their coracles upstream against the roaring current. When we reached Chusul, our *kobos* had to carry their skin boats back home along the river bank. Every boatman takes a pet sheep on the journey downstream. On the homeward trek the sheep carries the boatman's personal effects. Nowhere else in the world have I seen sheep used as pets and pack animals.

From Chusul to Lhasa was only forty miles, and we expected to cover that distance easily in two days. But the Kyi Chu was at its highest flood level in four years. Some of the time we could avoid the flood by staying high on the valley slopes. More than once, however, rock walls hemmed us in, forcing our caravan to wade into the river. Those were tricky moments as our donkeys struggled up to their big ears in water, with their loads half in, half out. We were not concerned about the food boxes, but to keep our precious film and recording apparatus dry we had hired four extra coolies. Ploughing without pants through the current, they were as funny a sight as the donkeys.

After a pleasant night at Jangmé in a peasant's home, we found the going next morning even more difficult. Many times the caravan had to be unloaded; it took ten coolies to move all our gear across the bad spots. At one spot the water was so deep that the smaller donkeys had to swim, and even the coolies had a hard time keeping loads dry.

The main road to Lhasa—Tibetan Highway Number One! Where it wasn't completely submerged, it was a narrow trail through the rock! Quite a contrast to the main roads leading to Washington! But then, everything in Tibet is well preserved in its original form.

Late that evening, as we splashed along, we suddenly caught a glimpse of our goal—Lhasa, far off, under a range of dark mountains—sparkling in the sunset; and the Potala, standing out above the city, its golden roofs beckoning like a far-off beacon. With great excitement we hurried on across the fertile valley, the evening air sweet with the fragrance of ripening fields of barley. But darkness was about to descend over the Lhasa valley. Our companions told us we must stop for one more night before entering the Dalai Lama's capital, the goal we had come halfway round the world to reach.

Only five or six miles between us and Lhasa! Too keyed up to do much sleeping, I lay awake a long time that night, thinking about all those before us who, in disguise, invited, or marching with the 1904 Younghusband Expedition, must have had similar emotions to ours when they first viewed the Potala from a distance and knew that a few more hours would bring them to the end of their long trek. Particularly I thought of Abbé Huc, compatriot of the Frenchwoman Madame David-Neel. He was hardly in disguise and certainly not invited, but after a difficult and adventurous eighteen-months' journey from North China, he reached Lhasa the end of January, 1846.

Huc was deeply impressed. He wrote: "The sun was nearly setting when, issuing from the last of the infinite sinuosities of the mountain, we found ourselves in a vast plain, and saw on our right Lhasa, the famous metropolis of the Buddhic world. The multitude of aged trees which surround the city with a verdant wall; the tall white houses, with their flat roofs and their towers; the numerous temples with their gilt roofs; the Potala, above which rises the palace of the Dalai Lama—all these features communicate to Lhasa a majestic and imposing aspect. At the entrance of the town, some Mongols whom we had formed an acquaintance with on the road, and who had preceded us by several days, met us, and invited us to accompany them to lodgings which they had been friendly enough to prepare for us. It was now the 29th of January, 1846; and it was eighteen months since we had parted from the Valley of Black Waters."

Eighteen months on the trail! Here was a man who had earned a sight of the Forbidden City. His tale is an interesting one.

Evariste Régis Huc, a Lazarist missionary, appointed to a Catholic mission centre in Mongolia about 1840, had a handful of faithful Mongol converts. Huc carefully studied Buddhism and the Tibetan language to plan for a theological campaign among the lamas of Mongolia and Tibet, but he made little headway toward converting them; most of the lamas he met considered Tibet itself the source of all religious illumination. Accompanied by his fellow Lazarist, Father Joseph Gabet, and a devoted Mongol convert, Huc followed all the way the established route which through historic times has connected Peiping and Manchuria with Lhasa. It is a long road—if it may be called a "road"—on which many physical obstacles and difficulties have to be surmounted, but it has always been one of the great caravan roads of the world. From the Chinese frontier city of Sining, Huc went to Koko Nor. Not far from Koko Nor and the Kum Bum monastery he and his companions remained for five months, from May until September, to wait for a caravan going to Lhasa. One thousand miles of difficult country, with lurking bands of brigands, stretched inhospitably ahead, and it was dangerous for a small party to travel alone.

Huc was able to join the caravan of the Tibetan envoy just returning from Peiping to Lhasa. The caravan was imposing—two thousand men, fifteen thousand yaks, twelve thousand horses and the same number of camels. The Tibetan envoy was carried in a litter between two mules. It was the middle of November when the caravan left the pasture regions of Koko Nor, began marching over barren windswept wastes and crossed the series of high mountain ranges in deep snow and bitter cold. Father Gabet almost froze to death, but Abbé Huc was built of sterner stuff. After grimly enduring intolerable misery, they crossed the last high pass—Tang-La—and gradually wound down into the gentler valley of the upper Brahmaputra.

Huc, like Madame David-Neel, arrived at the time of the New Year festivals. He encountered no opposition or unpleasantness from Tibetans during his two months in Lhasa. The Tibetan regent, an intelligent and remarkable personality, received Huc with great respect as a man of religion and warmly befriended him. But the Amban, the Chinese Resident at Lhasa, insisted that Huc should leave the country. Huc and Gabet were not ignominiously expelled, however. They left Lhasa in March in the caravan of a Chinese mandarin returning to China after some years of service as an official in Lhasa. It was a long, arduous trip through the mountain passes, and on one occasion yaks were used to force a passage through the deep snows for three days before the caravan could struggle through.

The missionary's successful journey to Lhasa caused a sensation in Europe. It was regarded as one of the great Tibetan exploits of the nineteenth century.

OUR FIRST DAYS IN LHASA

In Tibet it is considered good manners and good luck to end a long journey in the forenoon. That is why we halted for the night at a village seven miles from Lhasa, impatient as we were to reach our destination after toiling for twenty-three days over the rugged Himalayas.

Early the next morning our train of twenty-two mules set forth in the rain. We had only one day without rain in our twenty-eight-day journey from Calcutta! Passing a number of enormous Buddhas carved and painted on the cliffs, we rounded a mountain and at its foot came to a long wall behind which a vast, sprawling cluster of stone buildings climbed, tier upon tier, up the lower slope. This was Drepung, the largest monastery in the world, housing ten thousand monks.

As we rode by this tremendous centre, dedicated to lamaism, two men a short distance ahead on the trail dismounted and walked toward us. Naturally, we dismounted, too. One apparently was a Tibetan official and the other his aide. Dressed in bright red and purple silk robes and wearing a canary-yellow inverted-bowl hat, the official introduced himself in halting English as Dorje Changwaba. He announced that His Holiness, the Dalai Lama, had assigned to him the honour of acting as our host during our stay in the Forbidden City.

Dorje explained that he knew only a little English, learned from his late father, who was one of four boys who had attended school at Rugby, in England, the only

Tibetans ever sent to Europe for an education. It came about in this way. When the thirteenth Dalai Lama was living in self-imposed exile in Darjeeling to avoid capture by the Chinese invaders of his country, Sir Charles Bell advised him to send a few Tibetan boys to school in England. His Holiness thought that a good idea, so after his return to Tibet in 1912 he selected four boys of the upper middle class from the ages of twelve to fifteen. Accompanied to England by an English official working in Tibet and by a Tibetan official and his wife, the boys were enrolled at the celebrated Rugby School in 1913. One was to learn mining engineering; another was chosen for a military career; the third was to study electrical engineering; and the fourth, telegraphy and surveying. The few years the Tibetans spent in England were not enough for them to become expert in these fields, especially when the English language had to be mastered first. But it is pleasant to know that they made many friends, and entered heartily into the games, sports and fun of their English schoolmates. The lad who studied mining engineering set about exploring for gold and other minerals when he got home. But as soon as he started to dig, the abbot from the nearest monastery objected, insisting that he replace the stones and move away because the local spirits were being disturbed. After several futile attempts, he abandoned mining and went into government work.

Three of the Rugbeians died at a comparatively early age —some say under mysterious circumstances. Perhaps the more fanatical among the lamas did not approve of this new-fangled western education polluting their sacred land. The experiment was never tried a second time. We were soon to meet the sole survivor of the Rugby quartet.

We crossed the Kyi Chu River, which flows past Lhasa, over a modern steel bridge, strangely incongruous in this medieval setting of temples, *chortens* and monasteries.

Built in the late nineteen-thirties at the insistence of Tsarong Shapé, the wealthiest man in Tibet and one of its most progressive elder statesmen, the bridge had to be carried by coolies and mules over the mountains, beam by beam, bolt by bolt. When it was assembled at Lhasa, Tsarong Shapé supervised its construction.

The bridge was thronged with pilgrims heading into the Holy City for the colourful wind-up of the week-long annual dance festival then under way. Every devout follower of Tibet's god-king tries to make at least one pilgrimage to Lhasa each year, usually during some festive period such as the summer dance carnival or the three-week New Year celebration in February. Among those who come to pay homage are such zealots as "the kneelers," who make the entire journey from their homes to the capital on torn and bloody knees, and "the rollers," who prostrate themselves at every step, measuring each mile with the length of their bodies like inch-worms. Some of these pious and painful excursions take three years.

My pulse quickened as we rode through the Pargo Kaling—the Western Gate—an archway cut through an imposing *chorten,* and found ourselves directly under the Potala. That fabulous and monumental building dominates the whole landscape around Lhasa and always presents another fascinating perspective, no matter from what part of the city or nearby countryside it is viewed. With the gold-roofed Potala, the monasteries and temples glistening in the sun, the crowds of people in their gay, picturesque costumes, Lhasa seemed to me like a rich illustration from a medieval manuscript, magically brought to life. As an enthusiastic traveller to far-off places, I felt that I had come about as close as ever I would to finding that pot of gold at the end of the rainbow.

"There just aren't any words for it," Dad said, radiant and happy on fulfilling at last his thirty-year ambition.

Lhasa is truly out of this world, scenically, geographically and culturally. Standing at the head of a green valley only twelve thousand feet above sea level—low for Tibet —the city is almost surrounded by tall mountains, the highest of which looms up eighteen thousand feet. Even in the summer, new snow can be seen almost every morning on the majestic peaks towering toward the deep blue sky. To add to the splendour, scattered up and down the mountains are red and white monasteries, some of which cling precariously to rock cliffs like eagles' nests.

Dorje now led us away from the centre of the city, across several flooded meadows to what was to be our home while visiting Lhasa. He took us to a government villa, called Treda Linga, on the southern outskirts and almost on the banks of the Kyi Chu. There we found ample room and comfort both for our animals and ourselves. There was no plumbing, but we had long since become accustomed to that omission. Our quarters were spacious, clean and well ventilated by a multitude of open windows covered with cheesecloth.

While we were setting up our cots and stowing away our personal belongings, Dorje excused himself. He returned in thirty minutes accompanied by a half-dozen servants laden with presents from his government. The gifts were food and much appreciated, for we had become exceedingly bored with our canned rations. The generous assortment included a recently butchered lamb, several sacks of barley, trays of cabbage and large Tibetan radishes, and a heaping platter of eggs which, happily for our stomachs, were not altogether ancient. We were even more delighted with the tin bathtub Dorje sent over from his house. We had been more than a week on the trail since our last tub in Gyantse!

There always has been a strict rule that a visitor to Lhasa must pay his respects to the Dalai Lama before he sees any other persons of importance. But the custom is that three days, at least, must pass before he is permitted to enter the audience hall where the Tibetan pontiff blesses pilgrims, usually only from China, Bhutan, Sikkim, Nepal and India, the nearby Buddhist countries. Well, for the first time in Tibetan history—so they said—that rule was disregarded.

We happened to arrive on the eve of the final day of the summer festival. A Central Asian pageant, unchanged in centuries, this celebration takes place every year during the first week of the Tibetan seventh month. The real climax comes on the last day, when the entire population of Lhasa is entertained by the Dalai Lama—all the officials, their families, the army and the commoners. The Lhasa authorities didn't want us to miss the grand finale. So, for once, in this land where tradition and custom mean so much, they decided to make an exception. A breathless messenger in robes of red and gold brought the news. We were to come to the Dalai Lama's summer palace at Norbu Linga, Jewel Park.

The closing day of the summer festival dawned bright and clear over Lhasa, with plenty of sunlight for our colour film. Early in the morning we joined the stream of Tibetans on the two-mile procession to Norbu Linga. We rode leisurely past the towering Potala, dismounting every few minutes to film the colourful crowd in their bright, fantastic costumes. Never had we seen more photogenic people. Tibetan officials and their wives were riding gaily ornamented horses and mules—the men dressed in flowing robes, with yellow hats of the inverted saucer type. The colour scheme of their silk robes varied according to rank and office, some gold and blue, others orange and red. The wives, who brought up the rear, were decked out in long silk dresses of bright blue, with green and blue hats that had twelve-inch visors to protect their complexions from the intense high altitude rays of the sun. Some women wore on their heads wooden frames studded with turquoise and coral. Over these frames, which looked like antlers, they draped their long straight hair. The ordinary townspeople, proceeding on foot, were no less colourful, perhaps not dressed so elegantly, but just as gaily. Some of the men wore large fur caps that for centuries have been a characteristic feature of the Mongol costume, and many had on the curious Tibetan cloth boots with flat soles of yak-hide.

Now and then we came upon vendors selling small blocks of hard yak cheese, thirty or forty fastened on a string, cigarettes labelled "Virginia 10's" and hard candy from India. Every few minutes we were approached by beggars spinning prayer wheels and chanting their pleas for alms. Begging, by the way, is a recognized way of life in Buddhist countries. To refuse beggars is believed to draw a curse.

The entrance to Norbu Linga is flanked by two stone dragons. Passing under a delicately carved wooden archway, we stepped into a park of poplar trees and bright flowers. A dense crowd of Tibetans was gathered around an open-air platform about one hundred feet square. This was the stage, shaded from the sun by a huge roof-like awning, painted in glowing colours. A drama almost as old as Tibet itself was being enacted to the accompaniment of drums and cymbals.

Our guide, Dorje Changwaba, led us through the throng to seats of honour at the far end of the stage. There we sat under a canopy on divans covered with red, yellow and blue silk. We were only about forty feet from the Dalai Lama. But we had to be careful when taking our places. The pontiff must not see us. This was a matter of protocol. Since we had not yet been received by the priest king, we were not officially present. To our left, in the adjoining pavilion, were groups of high lamas. In the next pavilion sat the Dalai Lama and his party, blocked off from our view by a partition; but we were able to see his mother, brother and sister in a booth diagonally across from ours. To the left of the Dalai Lama was the pavilion for the nine Cabinet Ministers, wearing brilliant yellow silk gowns and red hats. More ministers and high government officials occupied the remaining booths. At the back of the stage and on either side stood the commoners and soldiers.

In front of us the actors were alternately dancing and singing—acting out their ancient tale. They drifted on and off the stage and props were changed without between-act curtains, as in the old Chinese plays. The narrative was so swift and complicated that even our hosts from the Foreign Office were unable to understand it all. But they were familiar enough with the drama, which continued without pause for ten hours, from seven in the morning until five in the afternoon, to tell us that it concerned a Moslem king and an incarnate Buddha. The king, hoping to kill the living Buddha, sends him on a dangerous ocean voyage to obtain sunken jewels in waters guarded by serpents and demons. The living Buddha is attacked in his boat by the sea monsters, but after a long struggle he succeeds in recovering the jewels from the ocean floor, thus foiling the Moslem king. There is a touch of Superman in some of these ancient Tibetan religious dramas! The whole plot was vividly unfolded by the actors as they danced and sang. They even indicated a boat going through all the motions of sailing a rough sea, and showed in pantomime the struggle with the serpents.

A gong sounded at midday, and we adjourned for lunch with the lamas and government officials. We ate with the Tibetan officials in a courtyard decorated with grotesque carvings of Buddhist animals and multi-coloured reliefs. Sitting Buddha fashion, with legs tucked under, we were served slabs of pasty yak cheese, bowls of rice and raisin pudding, and coarse barley bread. The meal was washed down with cups of Tibet's favourite beverage, thick yak-buttered tea. Then back to the play. Soon oriental hats began to nod; official stomachs were a bit too full.

Just as we were recovering from lunch, we were led off to another repast with Tsipon Shakabpa, Tibet's Minister of Finance and the leader of the first trade mission to the outside world in 1948. Rimshi Kyipup, lone survivor of the four youths who went to school at Rugby, served as our interpreter at this affair. When Kyipup returned from England he tried to develop Tibet's telegraph system, but the government at that time showed no interest in the project and he abandoned it. Kyipup has held positions as head of the city police and as city magistrate. Short and rather shy, with a deferential manner, he is married to one of the beautiful daughters of Tering Rajah, who is a member of the royal family of Sikkim. The Rimshi, with his good command of English, is often called upon to interpret at interviews between high officials and English-speaking visitors.

The Finance Minister seemed to enjoy talking about his trip to America, where he stayed for four months with his five-man trade mission. Their work, promoting United States-Tibetan trade, took them from one end of the States to the other. Tsipon Shakabpa had been utterly bewildered by our machinery, our trains, planes, autos and San Francisco's cable cars. He had high praise for the hotels where they stayed, and marvelled at the comforts and efficiency of the "City of San Francisco," which sped them to the East Coast. The Rocky Mountains and the Sierras reminded the delegation of their own Himalayas, while the Hudson River made them a little homesick for the Kyi Chu. Tsipon Shakabpa was especially impressed with the American universities he had visited, and hoped that his government would send a few promising young Tibetans to school over here. His only real disappointment in America was not being recognized as a Tibetan. He said some folks thought he was Chinese, others took him for Indian, others Japanese. But strangest of all, he said, was being confused with the British! It just goes to show how ignorant we Americans are about Tibet.

Tsipon Shakabpa realizes that Tibet must be brought before the American public and described to the world if it is to enlarge its circle of friends and win outside support in its struggle against the Red tide. It was this forward-looking Finance Minister's influence which enabled us to visit Tibet. He convinced the high Lhasa authorities that the people of America should know something about their country, both through words and photographs, and persuaded them to take a chance on us.

From luncheon number two we returned to our seats at the folk play. Shortly afterward, young acolyte monks passed around heaping trays of bread. How anyone could have a crumb of appetite after such feasting was beyond our comprehension, but we were obliged to dig in with the others. The bread was followed by tea. Incidentally, the average well-to-do Tibetan consumes his thick tea at the fantastic rate of forty to fifty cups a day.

A little later, still almost stupefied with overeating, we went back of the pavilions to photograph the army. A private show was put on for us while guards, wielding long wooden staves, unmercifully beat back the curious crowd of commoners to clear a path for our cameras. The national army then numbered about ten thousand men, but we have heard that it has now been increased to nearly one hundred thousand. It is the only Tibetan institution that has been changed in centuries. The Dalai Lama's troops, for the most part, are clad in native costume, but a few hundred wear the discarded British uniform of World War I, with rifles and other light equipment of the same period.

The army had three bands performing and a corps of bagpipers!

"Bagpipes in the Holy City!" said my father. "Great Scott! It's unbelievable."

"Just listen to them, Dad. Of all things, they are playing a medley of 'God Save the King,' 'Marching Through Georgia,' and 'Auld Lang Syne.' "

"And not badly either, considering how utterly different their music is from ours," Dad replied.

"Most likely the bagpipes and the old familiar western tunes floated into Lhasa on the wave of British influence that followed the Younghusband Expedition," I ventured.

After our special army show we returned to our seats to see the conclusion of the dance-drama. Three towering monks appeared. Brawny as professional wrestlers, and as tall as the giant in America's favourite circus, they were part of the Dalai Lama's personal bodyguard. The ground fairly trembled as this overpowering trio stepped forward, arms filled with *katas* for the actors. These white silk scarves, which the actors received around their necks, probably had money tied in them.

Again they danced, more wildly than before; costumes and scarves went flying in all directions. And as they gyrated they paused, one after the other, to scoop cupfuls of barley flour from a huge tub; then on they danced.

Suddenly all the whirling stopped. In a final, auspicious gesture the players gave vent to piercing cries as they tossed into the air the flour from their cups. Then, all together, they fell face down in the direction of their god-king's pavilion. The Earth Bull summer festival was over.

That night we put our portable radio equipment to work and made the first broadcast in history from Lhasa. This we rushed out to India by courier, and on to our radio colleagues in New York.

While awaiting an official audience with the Dalai Lama, we took advantage of the next few days to do some sight-seeing. Lhasa itself is a collection of white-washed buildings, mostly of stone and from one to four stories high, built along a maze of narrow, rutted streets. Around the city we observed fields of yellow grain and herds of grazing yak.

No census has ever been taken of Lhasa's population, but rough estimates place it at twenty-five thousand. However, if one includes the monks who live in the nearby hills at Drepung, Sera and Ganden—the three large monasteries often called "the three pillars of state"—and the monks in many smaller monasteries, the population probably comes closer to fifty thousand. And that figure is doubled during holidays when pilgrims swarm into the capital.

In many respects Lhasa reminded me of the Turkish town of Kars in the lower Caucasus, also in mountainous country and with narrow, muddy streets. Even the Kars bazaar resembles the one at Lhasa, with merchandise laid out on tables along the streets, shaded by canvas awnings and umbrellas.

The Lhasa bazaar attracts all strangers in the city— Tibetan country folk, Ladakhi, Sikkimese and Mongolian pilgrims as well as rare western visitors, like us. It was surprising what could be purchased in the Holy City under the awnings and umbrellas of the noisy merchants. Sun glasses, mirrors, cigarettes, soap, aluminium pots, flash-lights and toilet articles are jumbled together on the stalls with oriental silks, tea and jewellery. Yes, a few small articles from the West are available at a stiff price, since everything must be brought in by caravan.

These few products of the machine age, however, have had little effect on the culture of the community. For instance, nothing is known of modern plumbing in Lhasa. Those in the Dalai Lama's capital who bother to bathe— and nobles and officials do—use pitchers and basins. Refuse piles up in all corners of the city; once a year these offal heaps are transferred to the fields to stimulate crops. The odours of Lhasa are not entirely pleasant. The nobles usually hold scented handkerchiefs to their noses as they ride along. To add to this unpleasantness, dead animals are tossed on the refuse piles, to be fought over and devoured by the city's scavengers—thousands of mangy dogs and ravens. If it were not for the rigorous mountain climate, the strong sunshine and the almost complete absence of flies or other insects, Lhasa would have a major health problem. But the few unpleasant aspects of Tibet's capital are more than offset by its fascinating people in their attractive costumes, the hospitality, the gaiety and strangeness of it all, and the pageantry, which has come down in Tibet like a tapestry brought vividly to life from the Middle Ages.

Plans are now afoot for the complete electrification of the city. When the equipment arrives from England and Lhasa is lighted by modern methods, I imagine that a regular procession of electrical appliances will make its slow way over snowbound passes and across windswept plains. That is, unless what happened once before repeats itself. Some years ago Lhasa ordered electrical equipment, but the coolies lugging the heavy machinery over the mountains from India found that it was much quicker and easier to let gravity do part of their work—so they rolled as much of the load as they could down the boulder-strewn passes. Naturally, most of the apparatus was ruined beyond repair.

People of means travel about the city on horses or mules. The others walk. For Lhasa, like every other place in Tibet, has no wheeled vehicles. Even for heavy hauling, there are no carts. We saw a great deal of construction going on, but the stone and earth for this work are carried on the backs of men or donkeys.

Why, we asked Tibetan officials, isn't the wheel employed in their country as a means of transportation? The answer was typically Tibetan. We were told that even if the simple oxcart was used, Tibet's narrow trails would have to be expanded into roads, and roads disfigure the country and anger the spirits. The same line of reasoning seems to be followed here as on the subject of mining. Any exploitation of nature is undesirable from a religious standpoint. However, we suspected another more important reason for the absence of wheels. The roads would be a menace to Tibet's isolation, making it easier for outside penetration, not only by harmless travellers, but by invading armies as well.

We were saving the sparkling golden-roofed Potala for a special leisurely visit. Next to the Potala the chief point of interest in Lhasa is the Jokang, or cathedral, in the heart of the city. This great temple is perhaps the holiest place in a country studded with shrines. Under a roof lavishly ornamented with gold rests a huge, jewel-encrusted image of Buddha, brought from China in the seventh century by one of the wives of King Song Tsen Gampo. As I told in another chapter, the great king presided over the birth of Tibetan civilization as we know it today, and he was converted to Buddhism by his two wives, a Chinese princess and a princess from Nepal. The two queens used his influence to spread Buddhism throughout Tibet. Monasteries were erected and the priesthood established to lay the foundations for the Buddhist religious fervour so strong in Tibet today.

In the Jokang, Song Tsen Gampo's image of Buddha and other smaller figures are surrounded by scores of flickering yak-butter lamps. On the afternoon of our visit, groups of monks, chanting softly, were conducting religious services in the cathedral, which is the first stop for Buddhist pilgrims visiting the capital. The great court within the Jokang is lined on either side with hundreds of small cylindrical prayer wheels set on greased spindles. When the monks stroll by, they spin each barrel-like wheel until the entire row is in motion. The rumbling of these wheels, transmitting thousands of prayers to Buddha simultaneously, sounds like the roar of a diving roller coaster. Rats and mice run unmolested through the temple, nibbling at the barley offerings of pilgrims. The monks' belief in reincarnation keeps them from harming these creatures.

On the outskirts of Lhasa live most of Tibet's nobility, an exclusive group which seldom admits those of lower status to its ranks. They live in three- or four-storey homes, constructed of mud-cemented stone. On each corner of the flat roofs are festoons of prayer flags. The Tibetans love flowers, and most homes are fronted by flower gardens. This comparative luxury is in direct contrast to the way the commoners live in small houses of stone, or in yak-hair tents.

However, the residents of Lhasa, regardless of their status, are merry and hospitable, especially during the joyous summer festival period. Our excursions about the town invariably aroused peals of laughter from the populace. With our fair complexions, narrow, sunburned noses, and our sweaters, ski pants and boots, we must have seemed very odd to the Tibetans. Our manner of riding—posting in the saddle, instead of jouncing as they do—also seemed to tickle the Tibetan funny bone. But we had no objection to their merriment at our expense. It was far better to be so welcomed to Lhasa than to be confronted by the hostility that had greeted some travellers in the past.

12

THE FOURTEENTH DALAI
LAMA

ARRANGEMENTS were made for our visit to the Dalai
Lama a couple of days after the summer festival. We were
eager with anticipation at the prospect of meeting His
Holiness. No ruler, today, we reflected, commands the
homage and devotion, both in spiritual and temporal
matters, accorded to the leader of Tibet's kingdom in the
clouds. To his followers, the pontiff in the Potala is a
divine incarnation of Chenrezi, the multi-armed, multi-
headed patron god of the Tibetans.

In view of our coming visit to the god-king, we were
naturally interested in tracing back the sacred Tibetan
dynasty to its beginnings—reviewing in our minds all we
had previously read and what we had heard in the past
few weeks from Tibetans themselves about the Dalai
Lamas. They have a fascinating history.

In the fourteenth century, Lotus Thunderbolt, son of a
herdsman in eastern Tibet, manifested phenomenal spiritual
qualities from his childhood. He became a monk, an
ardent disciple of the reformer Tsong-kapa, who founded
the Yellow Hat sect. Known as "The Perfecter of the
Priesthood," Lotus Thunderbolt established the great
Yellow Hat monasteries of Drepung and Tashi Lhunpo.
Some years after his death, his spirit was believed to have
passed into another monk, who then became head of
Drepung. By this time the idea was firmly rooted that a
few saintly persons, through the holiness of their lives,

were entitled to pass into Buddhahood, but that sometimes they renounced this privilege to return to earth and help others attain spiritual elevation. However, the head of the Yellow Hats still concentrated on spiritual authority, making little effort to exercise secular control.

It was the third in order of succession, Sonam Gyatso, who received the title "Dalai Lama Vajradhara"—"The All-Embracing Lama, the Holder of the Thunderbolt"—from the powerful Mongol chief Altan Khan in the middle of the sixteenth century. Sonam Gyatso, regarded as the third Dalai Lama, expanded Buddhism not only in Tibet, but also spread the faith among the Mongols, who were especially attracted to the Tibetan form of Buddhism.

The fifth and the late thirteenth Dalai Lama are always spoken of by Tibetans as the Great Fifth and the Great Thirteenth. The fifth was Lob-sang Gyatso, born the son of a poor villager not far from Lhasa. He had continuous struggles with the older Red Hat sect, which refused to recognize his authority. In 1641, with the help of the Oelot Mongols, the Dalai Lama subdued the warlike Red Hats and elevated the Yellow Hats, his own sect, to be the rulers of Tibet. After this bloody battle—a strange occupation for monks who ordinarily will not kill even an insect—the fifth Dalai Lama started to build the magnificent Potala and made Lhasa the hermit nation's capital. It was during the first years of the fifth Dalai Lama's rule that Capuchin friars were permitted to reside and preach in Lhasa; Jesuit fathers came during the latter part of his reign. (I shall tell about these missionaries later.) Although the fifth Dalai Lama delegated much of his secular power to his chief minister, he was responsible for consolidating the country and centralizing both government and religious authority in Lhasa.

The thirteenth Dalai Lama died, or as Tibetans put it, "departed to the Heavenly Field" in 1933, at the age of fifty-seven. He went into exile twice during his eventful reign, once to Mongolia during the Younghusband Expedition in 1904, and again to India in 1910 when the Chinese invaded Tibet. Despite these enforced absences, he managed to retain the devotion of his people and ruled wisely until his death. During his two years' exile in India the Chinese issued a proclamation deposing him, but the Tibetans spattered the publicly posted announcements with mud and continued to turn to their living god in exile as the supreme authority.

For an intimate and very human picture of the Great Thirteenth the West is indebted to Sir Charles Bell, who knew him better than did any Westerner or, in fact, any Chinese or Asiatic except the Tibetan officials close to his person, and a few Mongols. Bell was in charge of the Chumbi Valley the year after the Younghusband Expedition, and from 1908 to 1918 he was political officer supervising British Indian relations with Tibet and Bhutan.

The two years the Dalai Lama lived as an exile in Darjeeling, he struck up a warm friendship with Bell, whom he consulted on many of the problems troubling him. And they spoke man to man in private; for Bell was fluent in Tibetan. More than that, he had a genuine grasp and understanding of the Tibetan point of view, and great affection for the Tibetans. In 1920, at the request of the Dalai Lama, he was sent in charge of a British diplomatic mission to Lhasa, where he remained almost a year, longer than any Westerner had ever remained in the Forbidden City except for a few eighteenth-century missionaries; but unlike them, he came as the invited guest and personal friend of the Tibetan pontiff.

Many Tibetans believe that Bell in his previous life had been a high Tibetan lama who prayed before he died that he might be born in a powerful country in order to help Tibet! When the time came for him to leave, the Dalai Lama could hardly bear to part with his old friend and said sadly: "We have known each other for a long time, and I have complete confidence in you, for we two are men of like mind. I pray continually that you may return to Tibet." They never saw each other again, although they corresponded and remained friends until the Dalai Lama's death. Sir Charles Bell, then in retirement in England, made one more visit to Tibet in 1934. He died at the age of seventy-five in 1945, leaving as his legacy to Tibet and the West several revealing books on the people, customs, history and religion of the country he had come to love in more than twenty years of close contact—a wealth of information on which all travellers to Tibet, including myself, have drawn freely and gratefully.

Sir Charles Bell regarded the last Dalai Lama as a selfless ruler who had died from overstrain in the service of Tibet, and praised the improvements the ruler made in administration and his determined and largely successful efforts to shake off Chinese domination during his reign. Before the Great Thirteenth, no Dalai Lama had exercised complete spiritual and temporal power through his whole adult life. Many of them had died "mysteriously" before they were eighteen, with the regent in control.

But in 1933 the throne, so long occupied by the thirteenth Dalai Lama, was temporarily empty, and all Tibet felt the void. Everyone prayed for his return in the body of a child.

When a new pontiff is to be selected, Tibet is thrown into an excitement and confusion greater than the fever which sweeps America during a presidential election year. Before an old ruler "departs to the Heavenly Field" he sometimes tells those around him where he will be reincarnated. Three or four years after the Dalai Lama has been placed in his tomb on the summit of the Potala, the abbots of the Drepung, Sera and Ganden monasteries, the oracles at Lhasa and at the Samye monastery fifty miles south-east of Lhasa, as well as other high officials, meet to decide in which part of the country his reincarnation is likely to be found.

There is bound to be one, because the Dalai Lama has pledged himself to dwell among mortal men to serve them, although he has won the right to rest in the spiritual world. The State Oracle is consulted. In a vision the general area of reincarnation is revealed to him. The Oracle's vision may have included a peasant's stone hut on the shore of a lake, a hut with a stream flowing by, or with a single snow peak in the background. Armed with such a description the Panchen Lama, if he has arrived at his majority, and other officials traditionally delegated to make the investigation scour the country. Eventually they find the spot and the hut or little stone house which best fits the Oracle's vision. If the peasant child living there bears some of the signs that distinguish an incarnate Chenrezi, such as marks like those of a tiger's skin on his legs, large ears, two pieces of flesh near the shoulder blades symbolizing the other two hands of the Buddha of Mercy, there is little doubt that he is the reincarnated Dalai Lama. But if there should be uncertainty as to which of several candidates is the right Holiness, the true reincarnation will unerringly select several objects used by the Dalai Lama in his last life. That is the belief of all devout Tibetans.

Usually three or four boys who fit the preliminary requirements turn up, and rival regions are very active on behalf of their local candidates. The high lamas pick out the one whom they believe to reveal the most evident proof of being a reincarnation of Chenrezi, but there have been times when considerable political pressure or powerful influence was brought to bear on the choice made. The boy selected is brought to Lhasa with his parents, brothers and sisters, who are installed in regal splendour. The father of a Dalai Lama is given the rank of Kung, the highest title that can be held by a commoner in Tibet.

The little Dalai Lama does not live with his family. He is taken to the Potala to be tutored and given intense religious training for his future role as god-king. Until he becomes eighteen years of age, a regent and the high priests rule for him.

The present Dalai Lama is now sixteen years old. The search for the fourteenth incarnation, as told to us in Lhasa, before we met him, is a revelation of the way Tibet clings to its old rituals and beliefs. Several signs indicated that the rebirth would take place in the north-east. It is said that when the thirteenth Dalai Lama's body was embalmed the face was turned to the south. But when the coffin was opened to put in fresh salt, "the Precious Protector" had his face turned north-east. Then, too, many rainbows and clouds were seen going north-east. The searching party went to eastern Tibet, to one of the many districts annexed by the Chinese during their 1910 invasion. There they met the Panchen Lama, still in exile, who gave them the names of three possible candidates. The first, they found, was dead; the second ran off crying when shown the articles belonging to the late Dalai Lama.

The third was found in October, 1937, near Sining, in the province of Koko Nor, another Tibetan region confiscated by the Chinese. But his parents were pure Tibetan, and his father a comparatively well-to-do farmer. All the signs seemed right. The leader of the searching party sent a lama disguised as a servant into the farm kitchen. The two-year-old boy was playing on the floor and, it is reported, he immediately said, "Lama, lama," and even named the monastery from which the lama came. A few days later he is said to have selected several articles belonging to the Great Thirteenth. The lamas announced that they found several marks on his body indicating that he was a reincarnation of Chenrezi, Buddha of Mercy.

Everything seemed settled, except to take the boy to

Lhasa for a final test. But the Chinese governor of the province refused to let the child go without an exorbitant blackmail payment. It was more than a year before this outrageous demand was settled. Tibet paid the blackmail and in September, 1939, the Tibetan search party returned to Lhasa with the child, who was immediately declared the True Incarnation.

At the Tibetan New Year in February, 1940, the fourteenth Dalai Lama was enthroned. Everyone at the ceremony in the Potala, including the British representative, Sir Basil Gould, commented on the dignity of the five-year-old living god. He had to be lifted on his throne for the long ritual during which the high lamas prostrated themselves before him, and he in turn blessed each one personally, with an ease, it is said, that seemed to come natural to him. Indeed, as the fourteenth reincarnation of Chenrezi, he must have had plenty of practice!

The young Dalai Lama is, of course, being educated according to tradition. He must always lead a life of celibacy; his brothers came to play with him when he was a child, but never his sisters. He must never drink alcoholic beverages, although he may eat meat. Learned lamas have tutored him from an early age and given him a thorough grounding in Buddhist theology, meditation and the Tibetan sacred books. He lives a comparatively simple, secluded life, as becomes a young living god still under the guardianship of a regent, but he has many attendants to take care of all his needs. The name he received on his initiation into the priesthood is, by the way, quite a tongue-twister—Getson Ngwang Lobsang Tengin Gyapso Sisunwangyur Tshungpa Mapai Dhepal Sangpo! Meaning in plain English: "The Holy One, the Gentle Glory, Powerful in Speech, Pure in Mind, of Divine Wisdom, Holding the Faith, Ocean-Wide."

All we heard about the Dalai Lama only whetted our desire for the coming audience. On the day of our visit, two nobles from the court—official interpreter Rimshi Kyipup and our official host, Dorje Changwaba—arrived to escort us to Norbu Linga, the summer palace. They were dressed in bright red and gold gowns, wore six-inch turquoise pendants in their ears, more turquoise in their top-knots, and all this gay finery was crowned with dazzling yellow hats. After a last-minute inspection and repacking of presents and a selection of our finest white silk scarves, our court cavalcade galloped off. All of us were mounted on horses and mules richly ornamented for this exciting occasion.

First, to clear the way, went the outriders, wearing their floppy, wide-brimmed brilliant red hats. They were followed by our two nobles, to whom all the common people bowed as we passed. The Thomases, father and son, were next in line. We were the strange individuals at whom everyone in the Lhasa streets gaped. Behind us came our three servants, together with the Chogpon who had guided us from Yatung to the capital. They carried our presents for the Dalai Lama.

For His Holiness our principal gift was a genuine tiger skull—teeth, snarl and all—set in silver and gold by a Siamese silversmith in Bangkok. We brought another skull, similar to the first but smaller, for the Regent. Also for His Majesty we had a folding travel alarm clock, a plastic raincoat from America, and a bag of coins in a white scarf, this last a symbolic gift expected of all visitors. It would be an unpardonable breach of etiquette not to bring gifts. Before we left Tibet, the Dalai Lama and the Regent returned the courtesy with presents for us —Tibetan rugs, rolls of woollen cloth and a beautiful Tibetan religious painting.

At the palace, we waited for the Dalai Lama in the same courtyard where the religious luncheon had been served on the last day of the festival. Nearby, outside the throne room, a group of perhaps a hundred monks sat silently sipping tea. They stared at us curiously. On the roof two monks blew eerie notes from three-foot brass and bone trumpets. It was not music, at least not the kind I was familiar with. They held one note for an interval of several minutes, before switching to another. Soon these small horns were joined and then replaced by two twelve-foot horns, which produced a low, thundering tone like the bass horn in a band. The latter instruments were so heavy that, by way of support, they were placed across a golden stand on the edge of the roof. This steady one-note trumpeting must have had some definite religious significance. Suddenly, a monk climbed a ladder across the courtyard and struck a golden gong several times with his mallet. This was the signal for the start of the morning reception.

A line of a dozen or so monks quickly formed at the entrance of the low-ceilinged, Buddha-decorated throne room. We were told to fall in behind them, followed by our servants with the gifts. After us came fifty or more Tibetans anxious to receive the blessing of the living Buddha. Inside, through a haze of incense smoke, we could see the youthful Dalai Lama sitting bareheaded on his high, cushioned throne. Bright-eyed and smiling, he was dressed in a red lama robe. To our surprise, he kept smiling throughout the ceremony—smiling at us.

In a moment we were standing at his feet. My father, who had been instructed to lead our procession, held a white silk scarf in his outstretched hands. In less time than it takes to tell about it, the Lord Chamberlain placed on the scarf symbolic objects which the Dalai Lama took, one after another. The first, shaped like three mountains, represented the world. The others were placed on the scarf and then whisked off by the Dalai Lama with such speed that we had difficulty in making out what they were. One was an image representing the body; another, a book, for speech; a third, a *chorten*, symbolizing the mind. Then the scarf itself was taken by one of the Dalai Lama's monk servants.

Dad stepped a bit closer, and bowed forward; as he did so, the Dalai Lama extended his right hand and touched my father's head with his fingers, thus bestowing his blessing. Then he presented Dad with a small red scarf. The same ritual was repeated with the Regent, who sat on a lower throne at the Dalai Lama's right. Now it was my turn. I went through the same procedure except that I did not have to make the symbolic presentations.

After the Regent's blessing we were directed to the Dalai Lama's left and part way back in the audience chamber, to seats on cushions. My view of the throne was blocked by one of the tapestried pillars, but by leaning back a little I could see His Holiness. He smiled and kept glancing down at us, obviously as curious as any of his subjects about two strangers from faraway America.

From our cushions on the floor, we looked about the chamber. Above the throne hung a set of *thankas*, scroll banners of Tibetan religious themes, each containing Buddha figures and conceived in the old Chinese style that emphasizes serenity and delicacy more than personality or individuality of expression. Seated on the floor on either side of the throne were six or more high lamas. Many other monk retainers stood in the background, and several giant monks walked back and forth—the same body-guards who officiated at the summer festival. The whole time we were in the audience room the prolonged rumble of the trumpets on the roof came to our ears like faint echoes from a Tibetan spirit world.

We watched the devotees shuffle by the throne, none daring to look up. The Dalai Lama flicked their heads with a tassel suspended from the end of a short rod. He blesses with his hand only monks and distinguished visitors. All common folk and all women, including wives of ministers, get the tassel. The Thunderbolt Sow, the incarnate abbess who presides over the monastery at Nagartse, is the exception.

As soon as the shuffling line of Tibetans had been hustled from the room, monks brought us bowls of rice. We flicked a few grains over our right shoulders; then took one taste. That was all, just a ceremonial gesture. The monks brought us a half-dozen bricks of Tibetan barley bread, which our servants wrapped up and carried home. We tried it later for lunch; but it was too rich and too strong with rancid yak butter for our taste. We also had cups of Tibetan tea, which we sipped once ceremonially. Before the Dalai Lama drank any tea, however, Dorje, our companion, was called forward to perform an ancient ritual. On his knees before the throne, he pulled a small wooden bowl out from under his robe. Into this was poured a little of the tea the Dalai Lama was to drink. Dorje downed it in one gulp. By so doing he proved that there was no poison in the priest-king's tea—a custom that goes back to the days when some of the Tibetan monarchs were poisoned by jealous regents or lamas.

After our audience with the Dalai Lama we had an interview with the Regent, the man who will continue to wield the power in Tibet for another two years, when the Dalai Lama at eighteen becomes of ruling age. No Tibetan is certain what will happen then, but if the young Dalai Lama continues to develop as he has in recent years, they are confident that he will assume absolute power, as did his great predecessor, the Thirteenth.

The Regent received us in a reception hall not far from the throne room. His Highness, named Tokra, is seventy-three years old but still in vigorous health and mentally alert. The story of his rise to power is unusual and typically oriental.

At the death of the thirteenth Dalai Lama, the Reting Rimpochi, Tokra's predecessor, was installed as Regent. He was twenty then, neither attractive in personality nor very able. Because of his love of cars and mechanical gadgets, some thought him progressive, while others, in the majority, frowned on his unorthodox tastes as those of a child intrigued by toys. A much more serious charge, we were told, was that the young Regent was not honest. More than once Chinese gold lured him into serving the interests of China. Seven years after his appointment the Regent had a dream in which he was advised to abdicate his post or lose his life. Whereupon he immediately became a meditating monk in Sera, one of Lhasa's big monasteries.

Then Tokra stepped in and took over the regency. It was not long before China, feeling the loss of its Tibetan puppet, instigated a revolt in Lhasa aimed at the overthrow of Tokra and the reinstatement of the Reting Rimpochi. The monks of Sera were involved in this fracas. There was considerable fighting in the Holy City —red-robed monks versus the government forces. The insurrection was put down single handed by Surkhang Sewong Chempo, the thirty-two-year-old son of the present Foreign Minister. Surkhang went to Sera monastery, put the Reting Rimpochi under arrest and, without interference from the monks, carried him off to the Potala. When the Rimpochi left the Potala shortly afterward, it was for his burial. No one in Lhasa seems to know how he met his death behind the towering walls of the Dalai Lama's winter residence.

We had that story in mind as we sat before the Regent, sipping tea and chatting politely about our visit to Lhasa.

"In view of the fact that Buddhism was introduced into Tibet from India, doesn't Your Highness think it would be a good idea for Tibet to send Buddhist missionaries to other countries?" Dad asked the Regent through our interpreter.

"A very good idea," the Regent agreed, and smiled gently.

THE FOURTEENTH DALAI LAMA

As we were about to leave, His Highness called us to his divan and presented each of us with a white scarf and a small red one, like the one His Holiness had already given us. Kyipup told us it was a special compliment to receive these red scarves from the Regent and the Dalai Lama.

Now we were off for a real photographic spree! We were in high spirits. The audience with the Dalai Lama was in itself a concession rarely made to outsiders. But we were given an even more unusual opportunity— permission to take pictures, both still and movie, of the young incarnation of the Buddha of Mercy. According to our guide and interpreter many long-established precedents were broken to grant us this privilege. Never before, they said, had motion pictures been taken of the Dalai Lama; never had any been taken in colour. Why were the bars lowered for us? Again because of the Communist peril and Tibet's desire to win friends in the West.

We hurried to Lhundup Gyatsel, a gem of a pagoda with roof of gold in the centre of a flowered pond in the summer palace grounds. There His Holiness awaited us. In full outdoor sunlight a slightly elevated throne was surrounded by shrubs and flowers. Having checked our light meter and determined camera angles, we gave the word that we were all set. Out strolled the Dalai Lama to ascend his throne. The Regent, the Lord Chamberlain and a group of royal secretaries lined up on either side of the young Dalai Lama. Royal gowns were properly adjusted by attendants. Then we began shooting from all angles with our four cameras.

Thirty minutes later we had finished. His Holiness had performed marvellously. He smiled when asked and agreeably changed position for our cameras. With these outdoor pictures, we thought the show was over, but it was suggested that a few pictures should be taken of the Dalai Lama on the throne, before which we had been blessed earlier in the morning. This was almost too good to be true! Although the throne room was very dark for kodachrome, we did manage to get His Holiness to stand in a shaft of sunlight by one of the tapestried pillars, where we filmed him talking to his staff; and I took several flash-bulb shots of him perched on his throne, wearing the yellow-peaked cap which is his crown.

We were much impressed by the young ruler. He seemed human, kind and gentle-mannered, and by no means a terrified puppet. We did not speak to him directly nor did he say anything to us except for a soft *"Law-les"* ("Yes"), accompanied by the Tibetan sucking-in noise of politeness when interpreter Kyipup told him our wishes regarding camera positions.

The Dalai Lama is loved and revered by all Tibetans. They believe him to be a great reincarnation of the Buddha of Mercy and of the late Thirteenth. They expect him to equal or even surpass his predecessor in wisdom, kindness and leadership.

13

THE DALAI LAMA'S FAMILY—
AND OTHERS

SHORTLY after our audience with the Dalai Lama, we were invited to call on the young ruler's family. His father—a farmer in eastern Tibet before his son was "discovered" to be the reincarnation of the late thirteenth Dalai Lama—was given a four-storey whitewashed stone house near the huge castle of his exalted son. There he lived in aristocratic splendour until his recent death. The house now belongs to the ruler's mother, who lives there with two other sons, two daughters and several grand-children.

When we arrived we found the same festival dancers who had performed for us at the Dalai Lama's summer palace, putting on a different play in the courtyard for the royal family. We pushed our way through the dense crowd of townsfolk and monks watching the show, and Dorje Changwaba led us up a dark staircase to the second floor of the house. Here we were greeted by the Dalai Lama's nineteen-year-old brother, Losang Sumten, in the orange robes of a monk. Losang gave us a warm hand-shake and a broad smile, and ushered us into a large front room, where the rest of the family was gathered around open windows watching the dance in the yard below.

After introductions were made, we took the whole family to the roof of their home to photograph them in colour. Most striking of this group were the Dalai Lama's mother, Dhekye Tsiring, and his plump thirty-two-year-old married sister, Tsiring Doma. Both wore multi-coloured silk robes and Tibetan fur hats and had jewel-studded charm boxes hung around their necks. These charm boxes—*ka-u*—usually set with turquoise and other precious stones, are standard jewellery equipment for most wealthy women in Tibet. They are not merely for decorative purposes. A talisman is frequently placed inside the charm box to bring good luck to its wearer. And if the *ka-u* is set with stones of good quality, it is believed to strengthen one's bones.

Now Dorje led us down to the courtyard to take some closeups of the actors and to make a recording on our battery-driven portable tape recorder of the weird music and chanting—fantastic and strange to our western ears.

When I walked out on the stage with the recorder over my shoulder, the tiny mike held in my outstretched hand, the play practically came to a halt. The actors forgot themselves and stood gaping at the strange instrument, while the audience howled with laughter. A new wrinkle had been added to one of their ancient dramas, and they seemed to like it. Some even thought the filming and recording were meant to be part of the act! Unwittingly I made quite a hit as a Tibetan actor.

"The next time these folks see that play," Dad said later, "they'll suspect the management of cheating them when you don't make an appearance in the third act."

We were much impressed in Lhasa by the expansive and overwhelming hospitality of the Tibetans. During our eleven days in the capital our hosts kept us on a continual merry-go-round of interviews, parties and sightseeing. Once you know them and have their confidence they open their homes and their hearts and can't seem to do enough for you. With the help of our Lhasa hosts we accomplished in less than two weeks what would have taken months in most oriental cities. We shall always hold warm, pleasant memories of the friendly, generous-hearted Tibetans we met.

Parties, reinforced with plenty of food and *chang* (barley beer), are the chief recreation of the people who live in the second highest capital on earth. (La Paz, Bolivia, is several hundred feet higher.) Since they have no automobiles, no theatres, no radios, no organized sports, no newspapers or magazines and practically no books except ancient scriptures which only a few can read, these gala gatherings, often prolonged for three days, are the most popular source of amusement and relaxation. In the summer season they love picnics, often putting up beautifully decorated tents and pavilions in the parks and open spaces around Lhasa, and feasting in the open for days on end.

Every night we returned with heads spinning and stomachs overstuffed to our quarters at Treda Linga. Since we only attended affairs given by high nobles in their homes or official government receptions and functions, the behaviour was restrained enough to satisfy Emily Post. However, similar gatherings throughout the country are often raucous. The object of every host and hostess is to ply their guests with as much liquor as possible. The party is considered a complete success only when the guests are in a state of complete stupor, showing that the wine was irresistibly good. If a guest is so intoxicated that he cannot rise from his chair, a ceremonial scarf may be placed round his neck as a compliment.

Most of our contacts in Tibet were with nobles and high lamas, or government officials drawn from both these groups. This was natural, both because we had been invited by the government and because of the short time we had at our disposal. Most of all we wanted to see Lhasa—and Lhasa is the official seat of the secular government, and of the religious administration.

The nobles, sharing important administrative positions with the monks, have great power. They own nearly two-thirds of the land; the remainder belongs to the monasteries. In their country places they live much as did the baronial lords of medieval Europe—in great luxury, but minus plumbing and other conveniences we in the West accept as necessities. The nobles maintain in their households several tailors and craftsmen, perhaps an artist to paint *thankas*, or religious scrolls, and an army of other servants to handle the arduous tasks which have to be done manually when no mechanical gadgets are available. So many domestic necessities—food and clothing, even the leather and rawhide from the yak—are produced on the estate, that most noble households are practically self-contained. Usually, too, the noble has his own private monk, who lives in the house, performs all the ceremonies of the religious calendar and is on hand to take care of the special prayers when any of the family is ill or sets out on a journey or needs to call on the help of the gods for some special undertaking.

In Tibet the nobility are almost a race apart. A wide chasm yawns between them and farmers, herdsmen and other humble commoners. The peasant bows low before the landlord or official and uses a different and meekly respectful vocabulary in addressing the noble class. The peasants on landed estates are bound to the soil much as were European peasants in feudal times. They make their rental payments in labour, crops and cash.

The houses of the nobility, built of stone around a central courtyard, are impressive. Storehouses for grain and food and stables for horses, mules and cattle occupy three sides; the family residence, opposite the wooden entrance gate, closes in the fourth side and, rising above the other buildings, is sometimes five stories in height. But few of these semi-castles have glass windows, an imported product, for the cost is prohibitive. Only in Lhasa do the rich indulge in glass as a special luxury.

In the country homes of the nobles as well as in the

Two young nobles, " George " Tsarong and Jigme Tering, pose for
photographs with their wives. " George's " wife, the girl on the right,
does not speak any English. The other three went to school in India.

Before the sarcophagus of the thirteenth Dalai Lama this monk prays, rings gongs and beats a drum all day long.

Shaped in curves strange to western eyes, this is the gold-encrusted mausoleum of a departed Dalai Lama.

Lhasa homes we visited, the finest and largest room is always the chapel or shrine room. Here are kept all the art treasures—mostly religious, of course: rare images of the Buddha and the deities favoured in lamaistic worship, some of them studded with jewels and draped with rosaries of glowing amber; new *thankas*, shining in strong, brilliant colours, and precious old ones from which the colours have faded; copies of the *Kangyur*, the Tibetan Bible, and of the *Tengyur*, or Commentaries; rare Chinese porcelains; ornate Tibetan silver teapots. The Tibetan host usually receives a formal guest in his chapel.

But every Tibetan has some kind of shrine room, even if it is only a few feet square, as we learned when we spent the nights along the road in village homes and peeked into the tiny compartments, where butter-oil lamps were kept burning before images of the Buddha and favourite Buddhist saints. The poorest peasant dedicates a corner of his tiny hut as a shrine.

The peasant women, as well as the men, are a rugged, hardy lot. The women, as has always been the case in the rural hinterlands of Europe, do the housework, look after the livestock, carry fuel and work in the fields beside the men. After my father's accident on the journey out of Tibet, his teams of bearers sometimes included two or three women. They were just as strong as the men, and withstood the rough trip without complaint. Along the trail on the way to Lhasa we passed many peasant women, square-set and well-muscled. They were not beautiful, but they had strong, determined expressions, and looked as if they could dominate any situation or argument with their menfolk.

In Tibet, unlike most Asiatic countries, women have had equal rights with men ever since the early days of Buddhism. Rockhill says that the pre-eminent position of women in Tibetan society has been from ancient times one of the "peculiarities" of the nation. This may surprise many Americans who have an idea that our progressive country was the first to promote equal standing of both sexes. Actually, some of our states are still in the Dark Ages as far as progressive legislation for women is concerned. Here's where remote Tibet is ahead of us!

When a Tibetan boy and girl marry, they do so on equal terms. Then and there an agreement is made as to what it will cost either party to get a divorce, should circumstance make separation desirable. If they do part, the one on whom the blame falls has to pay. The woman takes charge of the household and does the domestic tasks unless her husband has servants; in that case the wife supervises them. But the man does his share of domestic work, too; he often cooks the elaborate feasts for holidays like the New Year, and he does much of the family sewing, especially on leather garments. If a woman's husband is away or dead, she manages the estate until the oldest son comes of age. And with her menfolk she joins in all merrymaking and fun as well as in all responsibilities.

The only reservation which must be made is that few Tibetan girls can choose their own husbands. Their parents arrange the marriage, but sometimes a determined Tibetan girl in love finds a way of getting around this difficulty, even to an elopement, as girls do elsewhere. And one recalls that in enlightened modern France parents still choose the husbands for their daughters, partly for practical reasons and partly on the ground that they are better qualified to make a wise selection.

Polygamy is practised only by those who both desire it and can afford to support more than one wife. Many men in Lhasa and elsewhere in Tibet have only one wife. However, polyandry is common among nomad herdsmen and peasant farmers. When a girl marries one of these commoners, she is automatically wed to all his younger brothers as well. The latter may avail themselves of all husbandly privileges until they decide to get married and start a household of their own. All the children of such a union are the legal offspring of the woman's number one spouse. But in a land where nearly one-fourth of the males become priests pledged for the most part to a life of celibacy, it does seem unreasonable for one girl to be permitted to have more than one husband.

One would hardly expect to find a moral code similar to ours in such an entirely different land—in a feudal, Buddhist society. It was no shock to learn that Tibetans practise polygamy; but we were, though, rather surprised that polyandry, usually found in a primitive state of society, prevails in Tibet, which in so many ways has a high level of culture and civilization. W. W. Rockhill, of whom I have spoken in another place, offers an interesting explanation of the practice. In *The Land of the Lamas* he says:

"The tillable lands are of small extent and are all under cultivation, so it is extremely difficult for any one to add to his fields, which as a general rule produce only enough to support one small family. If at the death of the head of the family the property was divided among the sons, there would not be enough to supply the wants of all of them if each had a wife and family. Moreover, the paternal abode would not accommodate all of them. The secular experience of the whole human race showing that several families cannot live in peace and concord under the same roof, the only solution of the problem in this case was for the sons of a family to take one wife among them, by which means their ancestral estate remained undivided, and they also saved considerable money."

In contrast to the peasant women, many of the aristocratic wives and daughters of officials whom I met in Lhasa are beautiful, with light, clear skins and sparkling eyes. The women of the nobility do everything possible to keep their complexions light and smooth. During the winter they stay indoors as much as they can to avoid the

fierce winds that toughen and darken the leathery faces of
peasants and nomads. In summer they either carry parasols
to shield their faces from the sun, or attach visors to their
hats. Cosmetics, both oriental and occidental varieties,
are in great demand. Some women smear caoutchouc on
their faces to prevent toothache and discomfort occasioned
by the bitter winds, and also because they believe it will
protect the skin.

The gala costumes of both the peasant and the upper-
class woman are much alike. Exquisitely made of rare
silks and studded with gold and jewels, these magnificent
dresses are priceless. Every peasant woman of moderate
means has at least one such dress reserved for special
occasions. Every noblewoman owns many. The Dalai
Lama's mother, for example, has one magnificent outfit in
her wardrobe which could not be duplicated in America
for twenty-five thousand dollars. The most striking
ornament of the whole ensemble is the headdress. The
wooden framework, over which the long hair is draped,
is heavily ornamented with turquoise, corals and seed
pearls. Those who can afford it wear the characteristic
long earrings of gold, set with turquoise, pearls and coral,
and two or three strings of prayer beads around the neck,
of coral, lapis lazuli or amber.

Neck clasps, buttons, and bracelets of gold or silver and
the charm box set with turquoise or more valuable gems
comprise the Tibetan woman's costume jewellery. Those
who cannot afford gold wear silver ornaments. Even the
poorest woman displays silver earrings set with turquoise
or malachite as a makeshift, and perhaps a string of glass
beads. Sometimes wealthy women wear priceless hats
with rows of pearls around the crown.

Where do the Tibetans obtain the stones and metal for
the elaborate ornaments which are an essential part of the
costumes worn not only by the women, but by the men
too? Enough gold is still found in Tibet by crude surface

methods to provide settings; as for silver, most of it probably comes from China. Pearls, coral and other jewels come from India, Bhutan and Nepal. There has always been a brisk trade between Nepal and Tibet; the best lapidaries in Asia, the most skilful in cutting precious stones, are in Nepal, whence many of the most valuable unset stones are brought by caravan to Tibet. Here native craftsmen fashion the stones in the traditional settings and designs acceptable to Tibetan taste. Tibetans find turquoise in their own mountains, but some of the best turquoise comes from the Chinese province of Honan, and the Moslem merchants in Lhasa send to Iran for its turquoise, which is of high quality.

With the Tibetans, turquoise has always been the most popular and highly esteemed stone. They invest it with special virtues. In their belief, turquoise is a protection against demons, wards off contagion, and brings good luck and health. Large turquoises are sometimes engraved with a mystic incantation to give them even greater power against evil and illness.

In view of the emphasis Tibetans place on charms as a means of preventing illness, you may wonder what is the standing of medicine in Tibet. Any comment I can make is naturally the superficial observation of a layman. Besides, there are no statistics or census-taking in Tibet from which one can obtain specific data about medicine, disease or any other vital information. On the summit of Chakpori Peak (Iron Hill) in Lhasa is the Medical College, to which students come from all the large monasteries. Some idea of the status of modern medical science in Tibet may be obtained from the curriculum of this institution. The course takes eight years, and the students spend most of this time memorizing long incantations and spells. They do acquire some knowledge of the medicinal value of certain herbs, but they have no knowledge of anatomy or of the functions and positions of the principal organs of the body. A patient suspected of having a contagious disease may have his pulse felt at the end of a long piece of string.

Smallpox has made terrific ravages on the population, but they are slowly beginning to learn about vaccination. Musk, camphor and aconite, used in the preparation of western medicines, are also familiar to the monk physicians who are graduates of the Lhasa Medical College. Nevertheless, such concoctions as the urine and excreta of Dalai and Panchen Lamas are also regarded as efficacious cures for any complaint. Generally speaking, the Tibetan still relies more on spells, incantations and the exorcism of evil spirits than on even such inadequate medicines as are known to his lama physicians. Whatever the illness, lamas are invited to come to the home of the patient and read passages from the sacred books, especially from the book of prayers to the God of Medicine.

14

WE TALK WITH LHASA OFFICIALS

MUCH of our time in Lhasa was devoted to chats with officials of the Dalai Lama's government. But before I discuss the talks, I should like to explain how this theocratic country operates. First, it must be noted that nothing about the government is hard and fixed. The Lhasa set-up often changes from Dalai Lama to Dalai Lama. A description of such a fluctuating system may be accurate for only a few years, but currently Tibet is regulated as follows:

Because the present god-king is not yet eighteen, the age when he will personally take over the rule, the Regent governs for him in all matters of state. Under the Regent are three cabinets, each charged with different duties and holding various degrees of influence. The most powerful cabinet is the Kashag, composed of three Shapés—or lay ministers—and one monk Shapé, the Kalon Lama, who is the senior minister of the quartet. All functions of government—executive, judicial and legislative—are vested in these four men, who are appointed by the Regent. The Shapés, who receive an annual salary of twenty-five rupees (about five dollars), are wealthy landowners and financially independent.

Above the two lower cabinets in authority and prestige is the Lord Chamberlain, or Chi-kyap Kempo, who is the head of all the priest officials in the country. Both in that capacity and as a member of the Dalai Lama's household, he wields enormous influence and power.

Of the two minor cabinets, one is composed of monks and the other of laymen. The first, the four-man Yik-Tshang ("Nest of Letters"), appoints all monk officials and deals with religious matters. The corresponding four-man lay cabinet, whose members are called Tsipons, controls Tibetan financial and trade matters. A recent addition to these cabinets is a Foreign Affairs Bureau.

There is a National Assembly called the Tsongdu. Not an elected body, it is composed of several hundred of the more important government officials. It convenes on invitation of the Dalai Lama or the Regent whenever specially vital issues face the government. The Tsongdu has the power, seldom used, however, to vote out the Regent. This body rarely meets in full assembly but performs most of its duties through a large committee which receives legislative bills from the Kashag, makes certain recommendations and returns them to be forwarded to the Dalai Lama or to the Regent.

For every important government job in Tibet, two men are appointed—one a monk and the other a layman. The monk always has seniority, giving the ecclesiastical group the real control of the country. All Tibetan officials are sensitive to the wishes of the priesthood, especially to the whims of the abbots of the three large monasteries at Lhasa—Drepung, Sera and Ganden.

Tibet is divided into some sixty districts, with vague territorial divisions. Each district is known as a dzong, the Dzong-pön being its governor. The bulk of government revenue comes from these dzongs, mostly as a result of trade activity. The Dzong-pöns have to submit a fixed amount by way of taxes each year. If a governor manages to squeeze more than the required revenue from his district, he may pocket the surplus.

The country has its own currency, with the *sang* as the basic monetary unit; also, its own postal system. The mails go through on irregular schedules. Postal runners, carrying bell-decorated spears as insignia of their office, jog along the mountain trails in five-mile relays, with letters from Lhasa to Gyantse. From there the mail is carried by the India-managed "pony" express—on the backs of mules.

An additional, but unofficial part in the Tibetan Government is played by the various oracles or prophets on whose prognostications numerous decisions of state are based. Many such soothsayers thrive in the Dalai Lama's land, but the most influential is the Nachung oracle near Lhasa, the nation's chief seer. Once a month this forecaster goes into a trance and peers into the future to help guide the decisions of officials and the lives of commoners. Tibetans have great faith in the oracles and are inclined to rely completely on their predictions.

We have been asked by many of our friends what we did on a typical day in Lhasa. Let's take the fourth of September, for example. At 7.00 a.m., looking out at the golden roofs of the Potala flashing in the sun, we crawled from our warm sleeping bags. At that hour it was uncomfortably chilly in our room for there was no means of heating it, and the summer nights at twelve thousand feet are cold. It happened to be the time of full moon, which meant that Lhasa's dogs had kept us awake most of the night. During the day these scavengers curled up in the streets, but at night the amount of howling, barking and fighting was beyond belief.

"In Lhasa you'd hardly call the dog man's best friend," growled my father as we started dressing.

Our first words to our servant each morning were always the same: "Sirdar! Ho, sirdar! Good morning, how about some *gurum pani* (hot water)?" Usually a kettle for washing had arrived by the time we finished lacing our boots. Then it was, "Sirdar, is breakfast ready?"

The sirdar's answer was always the same: "Yes, Sahib, breakfast ready. Just now coming."

From Norbu's grimy, smoky kitchen the sirdar brought our stewed prunes, oatmeal with hot milk, toast and fried eggs.

After breakfast, Dorje arrived to take us on the day's rounds.

First stop was the luxurious home of the Finance Minister, Tsipon Shakabpa, the official most responsible for our permission to visit Lhasa, whom we had met a few days before at the festival luncheon. A fine-looking man of forty-five or so, the Tsipon is keenly aware of what is going on in the world today and of the problems facing his country under the present disturbing conditions.

Dorje translated for us as we consumed a few cups of tea and asked our host questions about trade. He expressed disappointment at the failure to make any headway in America with his trade mission. According to the Tsipon, Tibet's economy hinges upon its exports, most of them to the outside world by way of India. Wool is the principal export, followed by musk, furs and yak tails. Trade with the United States averages annually from two to three million dollars. But, the Tsipon explained, all this business has been negotiated through India, which, in the role of middleman, pays Tibet in rupees. This arrangement has not satisfied the Tibetans, who want and feel entitled to payment in dollars.

"Unless India pays Tibetan traders in dollars, we must find a way to trade directly with the dollar world," he said, through Dorje's interpretation. Even the remote Tibetans know about the present value of the American greenback.

From Shakabpa's home on the eastern edge of town, Dorje led us back to the Foreign Office, where we met the members of that august body, the Kashag cabinet. All the clerks in the office bowed low as their superiors from the Kashag entered. Only three of the powerful Shapés were present; the fourth had gone to the Chinese frontier at Chamdo to check on the Communist threat.

This important trio was headed by the Kalon Lama—Rampa Sawang Lama—the senior minister. The Kalon Lama wore no hat to hide his bald head. The two lay Shapés, Surkhang Sewong Chempo, son of Tibet's Foreign Minister, and Ragachar Sawang, followed. Their yellow silk robes were tied with red sashes. They took off their broad-brimmed gold brocade hats, which had red crowns surmounted with two-inch turquoise spikes, and revealed their official headdresses. Their black hair was tied with red ribbon in a double top-knot, with a turquoise and gold ornament fastened in the centre, and a long pigtail down the back. The ornament is a small charm box worn by officials of high rank.

The Kalon Lama spoke for the Kashag; Rimshi Kyipup translated. The two lay ministers showed great respect for his seniority. They scarcely opened their mouths and contented themselves with nodding at the high Lama's statements. After the customary polite questions regarding our trip, the Kalon Lama asked the question which seems to be on everybody's lips in Tibet: "Has Communism come to stay in China and will it keep spreading across Asia?"

"No one can answer that difficult question," replied my father. "But in my opinion Communism may not have a lasting effect on China's age-old culture and civilization. Chinese life up to now has always centred on the family and on religion and both are institutions which Red doctrine opposes. Even if Communism is not entirely cast off, China may modify it to such an extent that it is no longer a part of a Moscow-directed scheme for world conquest."

"We hope what you say will happen—and soon enough to help save Tibet," the Kalon Lama pronounced gravely, speaking for his colleagues, who nodded sagely in agreement.

When the Shapés took their leave, the two Foreign Ministers, Surkhang Dzaza, the lay member of the team, and the monk Luishahr Dzaza Lama, urged us to join them over cups of buttered tea. They proceeded to tell us about Tibet's two main problems: Communism and China. These problems were the main reason the Dalai Lama and his government had given us permission to visit Lhasa. By the lucky timing of our request we had been chosen to tell our countrymen about Tibet's international problems and to ask Washington what military aid the United States might be able to give Tibet.

In an earlier chapter I related most of our interview with the Foreign Ministers. They told us that Tibet had been completely independent since 1912, in spite of China's insistence that it was a Chinese province; and they explained why Red China is now bent on the military conquest of Tibet.

At the conclusion of their detailed account of Chinese-Tibetan relations, which was translated for us piecemeal by interpreter Kyipup, the Ministers, without any fancy camouflage, came to the point directly: "If the Communists strike Tibet, will America help? And to what extent?"

Tough questions to answer! We were in Tibet as private citizens, not as official representatives of the United States. Naturally we had no authority to offer them any encouragement. All we could venture was our belief that our country would be sympathetic, but that actual material aid would depend chiefly on United States public opinion as reflected in the action of Congress. They did not derive much satisfaction from that reply. It is difficult for Tibetans to understand the working of the democratic system, so contrary to their own feudal form of government.

Actually, we were asked the same questions over and over again in Lhasa. Monks as well as laymen were deeply concerned about the future of their nation.

The Foreign Ministers had no idea what type of military

assistance they need. I doubt that even the Tibetan army generals could put down their requirements specifically on paper. How could they, out of touch as they are with military developments beyond their borders?

The Chinese Communists, if they invade, probably will do so by way of the northern plateau and desert, from the Kumbum and Lake Koko Nor region. By that route it is about six hundred miles to Lhasa. The first two hundred miles would be simple. But from then on it might not be too difficult for skilful guerrilla forces to harass an invader, cut his supply lines and make his venture too costly.

The most important requirement, of course, is skilful guerrilla forces. To create these, Tibet needs arms and advice principally from outside. Arms would include weapons especially adapted to guerrilla warfare, such as Garand rifles, machine guns, mortars, grenades and mines. The kind of advice needed is technical instruction in the proper use and maintenance of this modern equipment, and in the most advanced methods of guerrilla strategy.

I believe that there is sufficient manpower in Tibet for defence purposes, if it is properly equipped and trained. Indeed, we got the impression in Lhasa that allied troops, beyond a small group of military advisers, would not be welcome.

If the Chinese attack, they will have to march into Tibet on foot. Trucks and tanks would be of little use in a country of ice-bound mountains, with no roads, and an average elevation between fourteen and eighteen thousand feet. The Reds may attempt to parachute troops into Tibet. This is a possibility, if Russia supplies the air power. The Chinese could wait for a day when the weather is perfect to fly in an army. The execution of such an operation would take only one day. The best Tibetan answer to airborne Red troops would be a formidable ground army.

Recently ominous reports have reached the West of direct Russian activity in Tibet. The rumour is that teams of Soviet scientists, disguised as Mongol pilgrims, have penetrated the Roof of the World for the purpose of geological survey and map making. Their activity is reported in south-western Tibet, in the Lake Manasarowar region near the borders of Nepal and India. The word is that the Russians have discovered large deposits of radioactive ores and, at the same time, determined sites for air bases that will be aimed at overpowering India, Pakistan, and adjacent countries once Tibet has been absorbed into the Red orbit. The altitude of the flat many-miles-long plain adjacent to Lake Manasarowar is not thought to offer any serious problem to aviators. Will this be the site for a great Soviet Tibetan base? Rumours have come across the Himalayas that Red planes have already been seen in operation there.

I am being asked repeatedly why our country does not lend Tibet a hand. My father and I have discussed the Tibetan problem with our government heads. This seems to be the answer. If the United States offers any kind of military assistance to Tibet, our country must assume the responsibility of maintaining Tibetan independence. But if the Chinese Reds called our bluff, how could we move an army over the Himalayas? How could we supply it? In the final analysis the United States is not the nation to undertake that task.

The latest news from our friends in Lhasa in the fall of 1950 was that Tibet could take a breather—perhaps until the spring of 1951—and that there probably would be no invasion until warm weather set in again. By that time the Tibetan peace delegation, now in New Delhi and led by our friend Tsipon Shakabpa, might come to terms with Red China.

As I write, talks are beginning between Shakabpa and the Chinese Communist Ambassador to India. As one Indian official remarked: "Both Chinese and Tibetans are experts at delaying things." The Tibetan-Chinese negotiations may drag along for many months, but there are indications that in any settlement Tibet will be permitted self-rule under nominal Chinese suzerainty.

The next official on our calling list that day was Tsarong Shapé, a former general of the Tibetan army. Now retired, and sixty-three, Tsarong is a famous person in his homeland and the wealthiest man in Tibet. The son of a maker of arrows, he started out a poor boy in Lhasa and wound up as the Rockefeller of lamaland. This really is an achievement in a feudal society that offers few opportunities outside the priesthood to a young man of low station. Tsarong, originally Tsensan Namgyal, was given his present name and title by the thirteenth Dalai Lama. The boy worked first for the official in charge of the grounds of Norbu Linga, the Dalai Lama's summer palace. Later in the service of the Court physician, he came to the attention of the Dalai Lama, who liked the boy's looks and took him on as an assistant valet. He became a great favourite with the priest-king and accompanied him in exile to Mongolia, when the British invaded Tibet in 1904, and to India, during the Chinese raids in 1910.

During the flight to India, Tsensan, in charge of a group of the Dalai Lama's troops, bravely held an overwhelming number of Chinese soldiers at bay until the ruler escaped. On his return to the capital in 1912, the Dalai Lama found that the head of the Tsarongs, the richest and one of the oldest noble families in Tibet, had been collaborating with the Chinese. Whereupon the ruler had the men of that family flung bodily from the roof of the Potala. Then he gave the women of the family, their estates and the Tsarong name to Tsensan, the young man who had saved his life and served him so faithfully during exile. He also made him a Shapé, a member of the powerful Kashag, and commander-in-chief of the Tibetan army.

Heavy-set, short, with a deeply lined face and thinning hair, Tsarong Shapé is the favourite of nearly all who visit

Lhasa, for he is a Tibetan patriarch of broad vision, great charm and a delightful sense of humour. Tsarong's house on the outskirts of the city combines Tibetan and western architecture. It was the finest private mansion we visited in Lhasa. Instead of being built around the typical Tibetan courtyard, it is surrounded by an attractive garden, beautifully landscaped with many shrubs, trees and flowers. And *all* the windows are of glass! Some of the rooms are furnished in western style, others according to the best Tibetan tradition. In his spacious, hospitable home, Tsarong and his family entertain lavishly, regally and frequently. His son, called "George" by his school-mates when he went "outside" to a Darjeeling school, is now carrying on the unusual family tradition of improving conditions among the people on the plateau. Tsarong does not speak English, but George acted as our inter-preter. Tsarong was especially interested in hearing our views on Russia.

"Is it true that the Russians have no religion?" Tsarong asked in the course of our conversation.

"The Communist party from the Politburo down to the Young Pioneers has only one religion," Dad replied, "the religion of Communism—world revolution. That is, if you can call that a religion."

"But how about the Russian people?" Tsarong con-tinued. "Are they told the truth about world events and conditions outside of Russia?"

Dad's answer—well, you know it in advance—was an emphatic "NO!"

Tsarong has always advocated the opening of his isolated country to western ideas and modern improve-ments that would prove beneficial. The more fanatical lamas, especially those in the three big monasteries near Lhasa, opposing any changes or innovation, are bitterly hostile to him. But Tsarong is courageous—did he not risk his own life to save his master, the thirteenth Dalai

Here the " Rockefeller of Tibet," elder statesman Tsarong Shapé, stands to be photographed with his wife and married daughter. Born the son of a humble artisan, Tsarong has risen to a position of wealth and power.

One of the many treasures of the Potala is this fabulous image of the Great Fifth Dalai Lama, who made Lhasa the capital and began building the Potala. The image is of solid gold. Before it is an offering of butter.

Lama? And he is tough-minded, too, under his jolly manner. Tsarong would like to see Tibet accorded diplomatic recognition by the West, admitted to the United Nations, and given assistance to develop an army strong enough to defend its borders.

To Tsarong Shapé the cause of the world's problems is greed. The ultimate solution, he thinks, is world government, but the time is not yet ripe for it because of the self-interest displayed by all nations. However, he is not resigned to the inevitability of a third world war. For, he told us, the rival powers may realize at the last moment that global co-operation is the only means to survival.

15

THE POTALA — TIBET'S VATICAN

I F all roads in Italy lead to Rome and the Vatican, all trails in Tibet converge on Lhasa and the Potala, the winter palace of the Dalai Lama. Before we reached Lhasa we caught a glimpse of its gold roofs from afar, and realized what the first sight of this building—one of the most striking and unique in the world—must symbolize to the weary and devout pilgrim who has made the long trek over the mountain passes to his Holy City. Even foreign visitors of different faith, like us, are thrilled by this soaring mass of red and white masonry a mile or so out of Lhasa, dominating the city from Red Hill, one of the many rocky hills that rise unexpectedly, isolated from the high Tibetan plains.

From the time of the early missionaries every Westerner fortunate enough to reach Lhasa has added his bit to swell the glowing descriptions of the Potala. No steel or iron was used in its construction, yet it is such a perfect structure that Spencer Chapman, member of a British mission to Lhasa in 1936, wrote: "The Potala gives the impression not of having been built by man but of having grown there, so perfectly does it fit in with its surroundings." One heartily agrees with him that it is a supremely great work of architecture, having an indefinable quality of magic. And as he says, "in common with the few unquestionably perfect buildings of the world, the Potala has some transcendent quality derived neither from the inspired skill of some master builder or craftsman, nor from its historical association, nor from the fact that it is the cynosure of innumerable religious devotees." Anyone seeing the "Palace of the Gods" would be aware of what Chapman calls its "divine excellence."

Every day in Lhasa we were conscious of the Potala. When we got up in the morning we looked out of our windows at its gold roofs, dazzling in the sun; when we rode home in the evening after enjoying the exuberant hospitality of a Tibetan official living on the edge of town, its vast white and red façade took on the appearance of an enchanted castle in a child's fairy tale; or perhaps because of its massiveness and a certain grimness, it seemed more like a sky castle of the Valkyries in Wagner's operatic "Ring." Wherever we went we saw some angle of the Potala, each more fascinating than the last.

Crowded as we were with interviews and parties and getting the reaction of leading officials to their pressing and critical problems, we were determined to devote as much of one busy day as we could to the winter home of the Dalai Lama. So we set off one forenoon to take photographs and make a tour of this fabulous building, the most famous in Central Asia.

Seen from a little distance or from the top of Iron Hill, where the College of Medicine stands, the Potala, in a vast circle of snow-peaked mountains and surrounded by a closer circle of green trees and parks, has an even more impressive setting than India's Taj Mahal, but unlike the Taj it is no exquisitely carved and filigreed marble gem.

What really leaves one a bit breathless is its tremendous size, the grandeur of its simple, almost austere façade and the way the foundations seem to rise naturally out of the rock. It is hard to tell where the hill ends and the building begins. The Potala is nine hundred feet long and a little more than that in height, from the street level—two-thirds the height of New York's Empire State Building. Indeed, it reminded us of an American skyscraper, towering as it does over the whole Lhasa scene. The walls slope slightly inward; and the long rows of windows, wider at the bottom than at the top, accentuate the symmetry and general effect. On the southern side, standing out above the immense white wall, is the central portion, coloured a deep crimson, signifying special sanctity because of the chapels located in this section.

In September the yak-hair curtains which offer protection from the glare of the sun are removed from the windows and every September, too, the white walls are given a fresh coat of paint. We did not witness this annual house-cleaning. The whitewash, mixed near the Potala, is carried in buckets on the backs of women and dashed up against the wall from dippers. The section of wall that cannot be reached from below is splashed with whitewash thrown out of the upper windows.

The celebrated Tibetan king Song Tsen Gampo—the one who was converted to Buddhism by his two Buddhist queens—built himself a combined fort and palace on Red Hill in the seventh century, but most of this was destroyed in later years by an invading Mongol army. On this site the revered fifth Dalai Lama began the construction of the Potala in 1641. It must have been as difficult to build as the pyramids of Egypt. For this architectural triumph was made with primitive tools—the same tools that are used in Tibet today. Each stone had to be carried from a distant quarry by donkeys or on the backs of men and women, one stone per person lashed to the back with yak thongs. Most of the actual supervision of the work was delegated by the Dalai Lama to his efficient Chief Minister, Sang-gye Gyatso. The Great Fifth died in 1680 before the building was completed. Sang-gye Gyatso concealed for nine years the departure of the Fifth to the "Heavenly Field." He gave out word that His Holiness had gone into retirement to meditate—an explanation both acceptable and plausible to Tibetans. This enabled the clever Minister to complete the Potala. The faithful were willing to do all this heavy labour—and without payment—for and in the name of their living god, whom they still believed to be with them in the flesh, but not for the Minister, important as he was. The residence for the reincarnations of Chenrezi was almost fifty years in the building—not so long when one recalls that the Gothic cathedrals of Europe were painstakingly built over a much longer period and that New York's Cathedral of St. John the Divine, started in 1892, is only two-thirds completed now, in spite of the advantages of rapid construction in our modern machine age.

The new palace got its name from a hill on Cape Comorin at the southern tip of India—a rocky point sacred to the God of Mercy, whom the Indians call Avalokitesvara and the Tibetans worship as Chenrezi. The Tibetans themselves rarely speak of the sacred palace as the "Potala," but rather as "Peak Potala" (*Tse Potala*), or usually as "the Peak."

The fifth Dalai Lama did live for a time in the completed part of the Potala before he died. And the Regent, his Chief Minister, also lived there while he was bringing the stupendous undertaking to its conclusion.

Next to occupy the sacred headquarters was the sixth Dalai Lama, the first and only one in the whole line who strayed from the path of celibacy and virtue. This was a natural consequence of the Regent's concealment of the Great Fifth's death. Usually the Dalai Lamas are removed from their parents at a very tender age and impressed by their lama tutors with the significance of their divine origin and the importance of their duties to the people. But Tsang-yang Gyatso—his name means Melodious Purity—must have been between ten and twelve when he was "discovered." His character and inclinations were formed before the high lamas could take him in hand. He made it his concern to beautify the new palace and he planned and constructed the Serpent House below the north ramparts. Here he indulged in life's most worldly pleasures—wine, women and the entertainment of dancing girls. Nor should one omit song. He composed poetry himself, mostly love songs, which are still popular in Lhasa. Obviously he should have followed the career of a charming young man about town, and not that of the incarnate God of Mercy.

Here in the English version by Sir Charles Bell are a few lines from one of his poems, showing the torment his soul endured in a godlike post for which his whole temperament unfitted him:

> *Dear Love, to whom my heart goes out,*
> *If we could but be wed,*
> *Then had I gained the choicest gem*
> *From Ocean's deepest bed.*
>
> *I chanced to pass my sweetheart fair*
> *Upon the road one day;*
> *A turquoise found of clearest blue*
> *Found to be thrown away.*
>
> *My heart's far off: the nights pass by*
> *In sleeplessness and strife;*
> *E'en day brings not my heart's desire,*
> *For lifeless is my life.*
>
> *I dwell apart in Potala,*
> *A god on earth am I;*
> *But in the town the chief of rogues*
> *And boisterous revelry.*

Needless to say, devout Mongols and others doubted that Melodious Purity was the true incarnation of the Great Fifth. He was finally seized and carried off by Mongolian troops, and was either murdered or died as a

result of the rough treatment he received. It is interesting
to note that the Tibetans themselves took no part in doing
away with Melodious Purity. The monks at Drepung did
their best to rescue him from the Mongols, who stormed
the monastery where he was in hiding. Even today
Tibetans persist in their loyalty to him and excuse his
disorderly conduct on the ground that he had two bodies;
one remained in meditation in the Potala and the other
wandered into the streets and dissolute byways of Lhasa
to test the faith of his followers.

Everyone who lives in Lhasa and all pilgrims to the
Forbidden City make the sacred walk around the Potala at
least once a year. It is a hike of several miles, always done
in the clockwise direction, with the Potala kept auspiciously
at one's right. As we puffed up the huge steps of the giant,
zigzagging stairway we passed a number of Tibetans
making the circuit. They were whirling their prayer
wheels as they kept reciting: *"Om Mani Padme Hum!"*

The Potala contains more than a thousand rooms. On
the lower floors are storerooms, government offices,
kitchens and living quarters for two or three hundred
monks, many of them young celibates in training, selected
from the sons of the nobility and official classes. Some go
into government service and some remain in the Potala,
where the Dalai Lama has his own private monastery,
called "The College of Victorious Heaven." Two of the
four Tibetan treasuries are housed in the Potala. One—
the Trede—is reserved for the Dalai Lama's private use.
Another, "The Treasury of the Sons of Heaven," is a
reserve treasury to meet the expenses of war or other
national emergencies. Everything from butter and tea to
gold, silver and precious gems is stored in the fortress-like
lower depths of the Potala. The accumulated contents of
these treasuries over the past two and a half centuries
must be invaluable. It is said that yak butter in the Tibetan
climate will keep one hundred years, but I for one would

not care to experiment! To add a note of grimness, prisoners are kept, sometimes for life, in the dungeons below.

Toward the summit are numerous chapels, great audience halls and meeting rooms, as well as the spacious apartments of the Dalai Lama and his close advisers and attendants. But we did not have time to see everything, nor would we have been permitted to do so, any more than a visitor to the White House can barge into all the private rooms and offices. We concentrated on the tombs of the Dalai Lamas and the summit.

As we climbed higher, we heard hundreds of monks chanting inside the vast building. There was the roll of drums, the clash of cymbals, the whirr of prayer wheels and the throb of deep bass horns.

Along the west side of the Potala are the tombs of several of the Dalai Lamas. The sixth is conspicuously absent. The shrines are built somewhat after the pattern of *chortens* and covered on top with heavy gold leaf. It is the pure gold domes of these tombs that glisten so radiantly in the sun, and they are the first glimpse distant travellers get of the Potala. We entered the sanctified chambers where the bodies of the Dalai Lamas are entombed in their two- and three-storey gold-capped pyramids. Hundreds of yak-butter lamps in gold vessels flickered in front of the crypts as the monks were conducting their services.

The tomb of the Great Fifth, sixty feet high, and that of the Great Thirteenth, even higher, are the most resplendent. From all over the lamaist Buddhist world the pious contributed generously to the building of the late Dalai Lama's shrine. The main *chorten* is encased with gold and richly encrusted in rare jewels, and the interior is filled with priceless old Chinese porcelain, jewellery, gold vases, and many other rare art treasures of Asia. Around the upper walls of the tomb a dozen of the finest artists in

Tibet worked for several years on a series of frescoes. Exquisitely painted, they commemorate events in the strenuous life of the thirteenth Dalai Lama—his exile to Mongolia and China, his flight and exile to India, the trains, automobiles and other strange objects he encountered in the outside world, processions of monks, Lhasa scenes and festivals as well as the Potala and other features of his life at home. Interesting, too, is an enamelled piece at the tomb of the eighth Dalai Lama, who died in 1804, showing English people and houses of that period—undoubtedly one of those done in China for the old East India Company. The Dalai Lamas during their own lifetime collected much of the gold, precious stones and currency required for their splendid tombs.

After we paid our respect to the tombs we climbed to the top of the Potala, among the golden roofs. The city of Lhasa lay at our feet to the east.

Directly across the way on Iron Hill rose the Tibetan medical college which I mentioned in another chapter. To the north and west, nestled at the foot of the mountains, were the great monasteries of Sera and Drepung, which we were to visit before we left. Many smaller monasteries, too, clung to the steep edges of distant cliffs. To the south we saw the Kyi Chu winding its way along the plain, making this district one of the most fertile in Tibet. Directly below us was a deep blue lake, with a small golden-domed monastery on an island in the centre. It was an enchanting, almost unbelievable panorama. Only the whirr of our movie cameras, photographing this breath-taking scene, reminded us that we were still creatures of earth, not of some mythical planet.

Below the wall on which we were standing we looked down on the winding road which is for the exclusive use of the Dalai Lama. He is carried up that path in a palanquin whenever he returns to his winter residence. Tibet not only permits no wheeled vehicles, but even the ancient palanquin carried by bearers is forbidden to all but the god-king, the Panchen Lama and the Thunderbolt Sow. The Chinese Ambans, at the height of their power, insolently arrogated it to themselves.

While we were on the roof we learned from one of our Tibetan companions that hail must not fall on the Potala or the Dalai Lama's summer palace or on the Jokang, the cathedral. Two lama magicians are employed by the Tibetan Government to prevent hail storms in and around Lhasa. During the rule of the thirteenth Dalai Lama hail fell one day on all three of these buildings. The late Thirteenth often had a way of making the punishment fit the crime. Because the magicians "neglected" their special duty, he ordered them to plant several rows of willow trees.

As we made our way down from the Potala, we passed a granite shaft. The top of this monolith had fallen a few months before. Our Lhasa acquaintances offered an interesting interpretation. They claimed that the Communists had been winning in Asia because the top of that column had been broken off. To us their explanation only emphasized again how deep and widespread is Tibet's fear of the Communists to the north.

16

RELIGION COMES FIRST IN TIBET

DURING our stay in Tibet we were constantly reminded of the importance of the spiritual, and the almost complete rejection of things temporal. Throughout the country religion is the strongest influence in the lives and thoughts of the people.

We saw Tibetans, our own caravan men included, pausing on the high passes to plant prayer flags and recite incantations against the evil spirits. On the trail and on the streets of every town we rode through, they were whirling their prayer wheels and reciting Buddhist prayers over their rosaries. Tibetans are seldom without their 108-bead rosaries. These beads are so much a part of their lives that they are used not only for praying, but also as abaci for counting and as costume decorations. Every Tibetan prays. Even five-year-old children commit long prayers to memory. The monk prays hours on end daily, but the layman, too, often devotes two or three hours each day to prayer and meditation. As I have mentioned before, the poor as well as the rich have shrines or chapels in their homes; and all flock to city temples or to nearby village shrines on holy days to burn butter lamps and drape white silk scarves over the Buddhist images. In every part of the country the Tibetans make the circuit of monasteries, *chortens* and shrines, prostrating themselves, praying as they go and turning every prayer wheel on their path.

OUT OF THIS WORLD

When we were in Lhasa, we often watched devout Tibetans proceeding ecstatically around the Sacred Way—the Ling-kor, or Park Circle, which includes the Holy City and the Potala, a five-mile stretch. Some fervent residents of Lhasa perform this exercise daily. Most piously obsessed of all were those pilgrims who measured the Sacred Circle by prostrating themselves full length on the ground every foot of the way. In some cases they had travelled the whole distance to Lhasa in this manner, hoping to wash away their sins.

The people, having great respect for their monks and whole-souled faith in their potency as divine agents, send for neighbouring priests to pray in times of trouble or illness, and ask the more learned among them to come to their homes and read long passages from the Tibetan Buddhist scriptures. Sometimes a wealthy man will pay handsomely for a group of monks to read the whole *Kangyur* aloud to his household—a session that takes several days. The family may understand very little of the sacred book, framed in antique and complex language, but a glimmer of the doctrine comes through to them. They feel that the whole household, from the father down to the family dog, has been blessed by the holy recital.

Yes, the very atmosphere of the land is permeated with religion. Happiness, prosperity and worldly fame may be enjoyable, but they are only fleeting pleasures for one brief moment of life on earth and therefore of little consequence. To the Tibetan it is only through faithful observance of his religious rites and practices—through being a good Buddhist according to the Tibetan tradition—that he can escape the continuous cycle of reincarnation and finally attain Nirvana.

Nirvana is often misinterpreted by Westerners to signify annihilation of the soul. Actually, Nirvana is almost impossible to define, but perhaps its meaning may be expressed briefly in the succinct statement of the world-recognized authority on Buddhism and Buddhist art, the late Dr. Ananda K. Coomaraswamy: "Nirvana is ethically the dying out of lust, resentment and illusion: psychologically, release from individuality, a state of salvation to be realized here and now; those who attain are released from becoming, and after death return no more." All Buddhists, whether lamaists, like the Tibetans, or those who claim to represent the pure original teaching of Gautama Buddha, like the people of Ceylon, Burma and Thailand, aspire to attain Nirvana, even if by somewhat different approaches.

What, then, does it mean to be a good Buddhist? While in Lhasa, we learned the answer to that question by visiting some of the monasteries high in the mountains rimming the town.

The good Tibetan Buddhist, like fellow Buddhists elsewhere who have shaped the details of their worship to their own backgrounds and traditions, believes implicitly in the "Noble Eightfold Path"—right views, right aspirations, right speech, right conduct, right livelihood, right effort, right mindfulness and right rapture. They also accept wholly the four "Noble Truths": suffering, the cause of suffering, the cessation of suffering, and the Eightfold Path leading to the end of suffering.

The Four Truths and the Eightfold Path may be considered the core of Buddhism, as the Apostles' Creed is the foundation stone of various Christian denominations. But before Buddhism was introduced into Tibet from India in the eighth century, it already had been transformed by strange Tantric rites from the pure ethics of early Buddhism, and then was combined with features of the native Bön worship, which is supplanted but never uprooted. So today the Tibetan Buddhist not only believes in Buddha and the doctrines he preached, but in his own living gods and lamas and, to a large extent, especially among the unsophisticated and superstitious commoners, in demonology, oracles and wizards practising mystic and occult arts.

In all events, the Tibetan realizes that, although spinning prayer wheels, reciting incantations and prayers, filling the butter lamps before the Buddhas and making the sacred circuits will assist him on his spiritual road, he himself must lead a good and generous life, one of brotherly love, in order to be reincarnated on a higher level at death. If a peasant adheres strictly to the teachings of Buddha and his incarnate lamas in this life, he may be reborn a government official or a high lama himself. A sinful life, on the other hand, will lead him down the ladder, to live again as a beggar or, worse still, as some sort of animal or insect. A better reincarnation in the next life is uppermost in the minds of the Dalai Lama's subjects no matter in what worldly occupation and pastimes they are engaged.

To help the four million Tibetans reach a higher spiritual level and eventually Nirvana, there are hundreds of monasteries scattered throughout the land—at least one for each town or village—with a total enrolment of about two hundred thousand. In addition, there are a few thousand nuns and, roughly, one thousand incarnate lamas.

These abbeys wield a tremendous influence in the government of the ancient theocracy on the top of the world. But of this large group, the most powerful are the three huge monasteries near Lhasa, known as "the three pillars of state." They house more than twenty thousand monks, a number nearly equal to the entire lay population of Lhasa itself.

The prestige and authority of the "big three" are enormous. Together with the other lamaseries, they own vast amounts of land, roughly one-third of the nation's eight hundred thousand square miles. In addition, large gifts of butter, tea, barley and money are contributed to the support of the monasteries by the government, the nobility and the peasants.

RELIGION COMES FIRST IN TIBET

Tibet is a poor country, and the monasteries are a terrific drain on the livelihood of the people. Their abbots are so autocratic that even the Dalai Lama hesitates to arouse their anger. The Great Thirteenth had courage, vigour and a strong will. The first Dalai Lama since the Great Fifth who dared to oppose the monks' abuse of their priestly prerogatives, he shrewdly managed to keep them from getting out of control. Acting both in his own interest as secular head of the state and in the interest of the people, he personally selected the head abbots for their loyalty and steadfastness. When the Thirteenth was only twenty-four, he seriously disciplined the abbots of Sera because of their injustice to some poor villagers.

Frequently in the past, monks from the top three monasteries have descended upon the city to wage war against a government of which they disapproved. The most recent instance was in 1947, when the holy men of Sera tried forcibly—and unsuccessfully—to oust the present regent and return to power the Reting Rimpochi, a previous regent who had been forced out of office because he favoured Chinese hegemony over Tibet.

We did not get to Ganden—"The Joyous"—founded in the middle of the fourteenth century by Tsong-Kapa, Tibet's great religious reformer. Ganden, thirty-odd miles north-east of Lhasa, noted for its scholarship, is a favourite place of pilgrimage because it contains the tomb of its famous founder. It was the head abbot of Ganden who was appointed regent by the thirteenth Dalai Lama before he fled into exile when the Younghusband Expedition entered Lhasa in 1904. And the regent from Ganden, far more a man of the spirit than a statesman, fixed the Dalai Lama's red seal to the British-Tibetan treaty in the sacred audience hall of the Potala.

We did, however, visit Sera and Drepung. It was raining hard the morning we left Lhasa bound for Sera Gompa at the foot of the mountains several miles to the north. The streets of the city were full of water, and people huddled in doorways to keep dry. Some of the poorer women wore large cabbage leaves on their heads to shed the rain.

Sera is the home of 7,700 monks, of whom one hundred are incarnate lamas, having reached the highest and final state of reincarnation before entering the world of beneficent spirits. The monastery itself is composed of a cluster of whitewashed buildings, rising tier after tier along the mountainside and climaxing in the sparkling gold roof of the main temple several hundred feet above the valley floor.

At Sera's gates we were met by two brawny, stern-looking monks, the proctors whose job it is to maintain discipline in the monastery. Wearing heavily padded red and gold robes, which added to their appearance of physical strength, and carrying staffs ornamented with gold, they greeted us without a flicker of a smile. At their beckoning, we followed them into the monastery. Ahead of them at some distance went their aides, who carried long willow staves which they used to clear a path through throngs of curious monks. The bystanders fell back as the aides, swinging their staves, cried out at the top of their voices, "*Pha gyuk!*" ("Out of the way!")

We climbed through a maze of narrow, winding streets and corridors until we came to the central temple of worship. Here we were welcomed by the twelve abbots of Sera, with heads either bald or shaven, and dressed in the dark red robes worn by all monks. They were elderly men from sixty to seventy. (We never found any evidence that Tibetans live longer than the people of other lands.)

They led us up several dark flights of stairs to their reception room just under the roof. We were invited to take western-style chairs at the head of the room while the monastery leaders sat on cushions below us. Usually a monastery visitor in Tibet may expect to be served large quantities of Tibetan buttered tea. We, however, were more fortunate, for the abbots brought us cups of Darjeeling tea and sweet biscuits made in India. While waiting for the sun to come out so that we might photograph them, we sipped tea with the head men of Sera and questioned them on various phases of Buddhism. They explained some of the cardinal points of their faith, stressing the cycle of reincarnation. They also pointed out that lamaism varies from Buddhism elsewhere principally in the matter of the identification of reincarnations. An example of this is the way the Tibetans select a child as the reborn Dalai Lama when the priest-king—"the Precious Protector"—departs for "the Heavenly Field." This method of selection was described in the chapter on the Dalai Lama.

After our friendly chat with the abbots, we were taken downstairs to the main prayer room, a huge hall decorated with delicate carvings, frescoes and numerous lamaist images before which yak-butter lamps were burning. This room serves as the main temple of worship for the monks, who also gather there at noon for their lunch of barley and buttered tea. We found more than five thousand red-robed monks engaged in their midday prayers and lunch. Seated close together in long rows, feet tucked under their bodies, they held out their wooden bowls to be filled from earthen jugs brought in from the kitchen on the dead run by boy acolytes.

While they ate, one of the senior monks, who sat on an elevated platform at one end of the room, kept up a continuous chant in a deep, froglike voice. The meal was followed by a monastic litany. The entire gathering bellowed with such gusto that the tapestried pillars supporting the high roof of the hall fairly trembled. To add to the eerie effect of this performance, the monks swung their shaven heads to and fro in a kind of mesmeric rhythm in accompaniment to their singing.

As noted previously, nearly one fourth of all Tibetan males enter the priesthood. There are two important reasons for this. First, at least one son from every family is expected to become a monk. Second, it is virtually the only way for a man of low birth to rise to any eminence in that completely feudal state. Boys marked out for a religious career are sent to the monasteries when they are seven or eight years old. They are placed in the care of monk tutors, instructed in reading and writing and made to memorize the scriptures. The little acolytes act as servants to their teachers. The chief requirement for a successful young monk is to have a good memory and commit page after page of the holy books to heart.

Some acolytes, never succeeding in their religious tasks, do menial jobs around the monastery and work in the kitchen over the gigantic cauldrons in which the tea is brewed. Others may show aptitude for art or for the masked mystery dances. If so, these or other special talents are encouraged. Some go to the school for medicine in Lhasa. Others rise to high positions in their own monasteries or in the government. And there are always some who take seriously to the contemplative life of deep meditation and study. There is no lack of opportunity for a gifted young boy to rise in some branch of the expansive monasticism which firmly holds Tibet because the Tibetans themselves regard the monks as a major element of their religion.

Determined to see as much of Tibet's religious life as we could, we set out the next morning on the four-mile trek along the Kyi Chu to the largest monastery in the world, Drepung, the "Rice Heap." Drepung was founded early in the fifteenth century by Tsong Kapa's chief disciple and successor, who later built at Shigatse the monastery of Tashi Lhunpo, seat of the Panchen Lamas. At Drepung is still preserved the fifth Dalai Lama's room, which he used when he was building the Potala.

RELIGION COMES FIRST IN TIBET

The monks at Drepung have often been turbulent, arrogant and warlike, but they have been loyal Tibetan nationalists, whereas Tashi Lhunpo has often leaned to China's side.

Like most Tibetan monasteries, Drepung is perched on a mountain-slope—a dense, seemingly unplanned tangle of great white blocks separated by narrow cobblestone alleyways. This vast mass of whitewashed buildings, with trimmings of red-dyed willow twigs edging the roofs and gold turrets above, is really a city in itself, supporting, as it does, more than ten thousand monks.

As at Sera, we were met at Drepung's lower gate by two giant proctors. A long tortuous climb, up flights of stairs and fixed ladders, brought us to the monastery's central building and the sunlit reception chamber, where the heads of Drepung awaited us. Cups of tea were brought in as we took our seats. Along with the tea came bowls of ceremonial rice from which we were required to take only a small pinch, to scatter as a tribute to the gods. Before us sat ten red-robed, bald-pated abbots, the solemn executives of Drepung. Their faces were wrinkled with age, eyes set in a permanent squint from years of reading the scriptures.

The abbots explained, through a spokesman, that they were not incarnate lamas. The latter spend all their time and energy on purely religious matters. The abbots, on the other hand, are monks with executive and political power. Their influence in matters of state frequently is tremendous. It is said that these men, along with the leaders at Sera and Ganden, represent the power behind the throne. They are, in effect, the real rulers of Tibet—they and a few score lay nobles.

So, it was with a great deal of curiosity and interest that we talked to them that morning. Here, perhaps, was a chance to absorb knowledge from the hierarchy of Himalayan wisdom.

What had they heard of America? Only that it is the world's richest and most powerful nation—the home of invention and a land of skyscrapers and lush orchards.

Lobsang Tashi, Drepung's seventy-three-year-old senior abbot, told us he had heard that a large number of fellow Buddhists were doing good work in America. He expressed hope that America eventually would go entirely Buddhist. To his pious Buddhist sentiments we made no comment.

I had been waiting a long time to ask Tibet's holy men their opinion of a subject much discussed back home. Isolated as they are in their mountain kingdom, undisturbed in their monasteries by war, unrest and the turmoil of modern civilization, they must have ample opportunity to reflect on the madness of the rest of the world. When there was an opening I popped the abbots my big question. What did they think of world government as a solution to the problem of war and fear?

World government, the abbot spokesman said, is a noble idea. However, a study of the Buddhist scriptures indicates that it is not likely to work. India had been peaceful and content in the days of Lord Buddha. And wasn't that tranquillity shattered with the advent of rival kingdoms? No, as long as there are rival powers, world government cannot succeed! Peace will descend upon the world only when men understand their inner minds, when they come to know themselves and, with the death of greed, begin to consider and help others.

The most articulate of our Drepung hosts, Lobsang Jungne, went on to say that there must be many unrecognized incarnate Buddhas at large in the world—all of them, of course, doing mankind a service. "For instance," he smiled, "take your own President—undoubtedly he is a living Buddha."

President Harry S. Truman—a living Buddha in the White House. Now that's an original thought!

But not all monks live in the large monasteries in and around Lhasa, Shigatse, Gyantse, and other busy centres of religious life. Scattered everywhere are small monasteries perched on the edge of cliffs in isolated mountain regions, with sublime views and undisturbed serenity to inspire spiritual growth. Then there are the lamas and monks who become hermits, living completely shut in darkness, with a boulder closing the opening of their caves. Some try this hard discipline for three months or three years. Through a tiny opening, their followers pass them a meagre bowl of buttered tea and barley each day. Those who attend the hermits are usually from a nearby monastery. A few of these ascetics remain until they die, never venturing outside, never speaking again.

"One day when I knock," said a Tibetan, holding a cup of buttered tea before such a shrine, "there will be no answer and no hand will appear to take what I offer."

When a hermit does not take the proffered meal, his attendants wait a few days, continuing to bring food; then, certain that he is dead, they open the cave and reverently take out the pitifully emaciated body, which is accorded the honours due a holy man. It is then carried high up in the mountains, where, with great skill and ceremony, it is dismembered and the remains tossed to the ever-waiting vultures. Not only hermits, but most of the dead are disposed of in this manner. Since much of Tibet is rock, or frozen rock-hard most of the year, few corpses are buried. And up above the timber line, fuel is too precious to waste in cremations.

Many Americans are curious to know whether we witnessed any manifestations of the magical rites, flying through the air, oracles giving out amazing prophecies in a state of trance—all the mystical attributes which they have somehow associated with Tibet. Frankly, we did not. All I can say is that the simple Tibetan peasant is superstitious and credulous and can tell endless tales of fabulous happenings. But he is also deeply religious in a sincere sense. From this distance, surrounded by all the unrest of the world, I can still close my eyes and hear the murmuring cadence of that ever-repeated prayer: *"Om Mani Padme Hum!"*

There are no European missionaries in Tibet today. There were some, however, a couple of centuries ago. As a matter of fact, Roman Catholic missionaries were the first Westerners to reach the Forbidden Land. Oddly enough, they had no special difficulty with the rulers of Tibet, although the monks were not always too friendly.

Friar Odoric is said to have reached Lhasa from Cathay in 1328, but with no authentic record of his journey available the claim has been generally discredited. The honour of being the first European in Tibet goes to a Portuguese Jesuit, Father Antonio de Andrada, who was permitted to establish a mission in western Tibet in 1626. After many vicissitudes and hardships had been endured by Andrada and his little band, the mission was abandoned a few years later.

The first European to reach Lhasa was Johann Grueber, an Austrian Jesuit, who had as his companion a Belgian Jesuit named Albert D'Orville. Father Grueber, who had been mathematical assistant to the Manchu Court at Peiping, was not making the journey for missionary work. The usual sea route from China to Europe via Portuguese-controlled Macao was at that time under blockade by the Dutch, and Grueber set out to find a new good overland route from China to Europe by way of Lhasa. Leaving Peiping in April, 1661, Grueber and the Belgian took the usual caravan route to Sining on China's western frontier. Then by way of Koko Nor Lake they followed one of the famous old caravan roads, reaching Lhasa three months later. No one annoyed or troubled them along the way or in the Holy City. It was, however, a very arduous and difficult trip, with many natural obstacles.

The two Jesuits spent a month in Lhasa, but they did not meet the Dalai Lama because they made it very clear that they would not prostrate themselves before Tibet's Number One living god. During their stay in Lhasa Grueber made many sketches and drawings of people, costumes, the Potala and other buildings which were later published.

Following a south-westerly course across the mountains at the worst season of the year, they eventually arrived in Nepal. In Katmandu, the capital of the little Himalayan kingdom, hermetically sealed against visitors in our day they were well received. They reached Agra in India in April, 1662, almost a year after they had left Peiping. There poor D'Orville died almost immediately from the hardships he had endured on the trip. Grueber went on alone to Europe with his astronomical and geographical findings. Grueber was the first real geographer to enter Tibet. Considering the crudity of his instruments, the accuracy of his observations is a remarkable scientific achievement.

Next came the Capuchins in 1708. They already had a mission station in Nepal. Eager to bring their Christian message to new pastures, four Capuchin friars pushed forward into Tibet and in two months reached Lhasa without molestation. Outstanding among them was Father Orazio della Penna, sometimes called the Livingstone of Tibet.

The missionaries had many ups and downs. They were begrudged support from Rome by their superiors, who felt that the tangible results in conversions did not warrant much expenditure. But the Capuchins succeeded in winning the support of influential Tibetan officials and were granted permission in 1725 to build a small monastery and church in Lhasa—the first and only Christian church ever erected in the sacred capital.

While this church was being built, the Kyi Chu River, flowing past Lhasa, burst its banks in the summer rains and flooded the city. Hostile lama monks, together with the people, blamed the flood on the intrusion of the foreign priests and set off to mob them. But the Capuchins quelled the riot by showing their yellow satin documents, impressively stamped with the seals of the Dalai Lama and the King. Following that incident the King issued a proclamation making it a penal offence to injure the missionaries or their property and stating that the floods were not due to the presence of the Capuchins, but to the sins of the Tibetans themselves.

Another annoyance was the claim put forward by the Jesuits that they had a prior right to establish missions in Tibet. Rome eventually settled the controversy in favour of the Capuchins.

Internal political dissensions in Tibet reacted unfavourably on the tiny mission. Hundreds of Buddhist priests from the monasteries in and near Lhasa stormed the palace and censured the King for his partiality toward the outsiders. The King, not daring to incur the ill-will of the powerful Tibetan monks, withdrew his support from the Capuchins. They were ridiculed and insulted in the streets.

The missionaries stayed on for a time, but they could make no progress in their work. They had been stout-hearted even to attempt to set up a Christian centre in the very stronghold of Tibetan Buddhism. Finally, the Prefect, Father Orazio della Penna, worn with age and the fatigues of his missionary labours, reluctantly decided to leave with his two remaining assistants. The Capuchin mission was closed in 1745. Not a trace of it now remains. Six weeks later the broken-spirited della Penna died at the Capuchin mission in Nepal. He had spent twenty-two years in Tibet.

Another early European visitor was Ippolito Desideri, a Jesuit who had been commissioned by his superiors to look into the matter of reopening the Jesuit missionary contacts with Tibet, which had terminated almost a century before. After a two-months' stay at Leh in Kashmir, he set out on his strenuous journey across the Tibetan highlands, and six months later, in March, 1716, the glistening roofs of the Potala were a welcome sight to his travel-weary eyes. The Capuchin mission was temporarily closed when he arrived. But he was most favourably received by the King and the Prime Minister "as a lama and doctor of law from a far-off country" and given permission to preach and even to buy a house, an exceptional favour to a foreigner.

Desideri settled down to a concentrated study of the language and also of the religion so that he could write in Tibetan a refutation of its "errors" from his point of view and a defence of the Catholic religion. It is amazing to learn how graciously he was helped in his studies by the lamas themselves. Their attitude was most tolerant, considering that the Jesuit's main objective was to uproot their Buddhist faith. He was invited to the famous Sera monastery, where he was given a house and permitted to build a chapel and celebrate mass. He even debated with the monks on religious matters.

Desideri did write his book in Tibetan and, according to him, it caused a great stir. Learned monks from the Tibetan monasteries and universities came to his house to see and read the book. Desideri dedicated the book to the King, who, he reports, received it at a formal public audience and had it read aloud. The maxims and principles, the learned lamas and doctors ultimately decided, were well set forth, but entirely opposed to their own dogmas and beliefs.

In 1721, a letter two years on its way reached Desideri with orders from Rome that he was to leave Tibet. He had been there five years, and during much of that time had lived amicably with the Capuchins, in spite of the conflict with the Jesuits, which had its origin in Rome. His account of Tibetan customs, religion and history was the most complete and important written by any European up to that time.

17

TWO BRITONS IN TIBET

FOUR Europeans live in Tibet. They live there as the Tibetans do and thoroughly enjoy the country, the people and the Tibetan way of life—so much more relaxed and tranquil than our western hustle and bustle, which often results in high blood pressure and premature heart attacks.

The first European is a genial Londoner, born within sound of the Bow Church bells. Reginald Fox says he has found his Shangri-La in Lhasa and will never again return to England. He has been in Tibet longer than any other European. Indeed, for all practical purposes he may be regarded now as a Tibetan rather than as an Englishman.

Fox has a Tibetan wife and four children. The three oldest—two boys and a girl—are at school in India. Since a knowledge of foreign languages is rare in Tibet and sorely needed at the present time, Reggie Fox's Anglo-Tibetan sons may someday hold high positions under the Dalai Lama.

At the outbreak of World War I in 1914 Reggie joined the British Army. Then only fourteen years old, he had to lie about his age. But he managed to get to France with "Kitchener's Mob." For four and a half years he was a despatch rider. During that time he acquired an excellent working knowledge of wireless. Upon his return to London at the end of the war, he was ordered to duty in the Middle East. For three and a half years he was "in communications" at Baghdad. From there he was transferred to India, this time with the Anglo-Indian railway system.

One day, fourteen years ago, he was asked if he would like to take a job with a British mission leaving for Tibet. He jumped at the chance, and he has remained there ever since.

As time went by, Reggie decided it would be sensible to marry a Tibetan girl. He resigned from his job with the government of India and accepted a Lhasa post under the Dalai Lama.

As I have mentioned, although the Tibetans are still firm in their desire to keep their country closed, they are becoming more sensitive to the global changes that have taken place in recent years. For purposes of defence they realize they must keep in touch with what is going on outside.

During World War II our American forces in India presented the Dalai Lama with a radio set that can pick up most of the important stations in the world. That's where Reggie Fox fits into the picture. One of his jobs is to monitor these stations, such as Radio Peiping, Radio Moscow, B.B.C., Voice of America, Radio Tokyo, Radio Delhi. Each morning Reggie provides the Dalai Lama's government with a digest of the latest headline developments and news of special interest to Tibet.

Fox serves an even more important function in his management of internal communications. Over the years he has trained and equipped a corps of Tibetan radio operators. Thanks to his tireless efforts Tibet has stations today at all strategic points, especially along the Chinese frontier. His station in Lhasa is the nerve centre of the whole system and the government's only rapid means of communication. The Tibetans must have someone they can trust on confidential government assignments. After all these years they have complete confidence in London-born Reggie Fox.

As we sat with him, trying to get news from home via the Voice of America, we discovered what a thorough job of jamming the Communists are doing. Invariably, they completely blotted out the American news programmes on all frequencies. We also watched Reggie put in a call to Bob Ford, his colleague in Tibet, another Englishman. Ford, an ex-R.A.F. radio operator, arrived recently. Fox brought him over and stationed him, equipped with a portable radio outfit, at a particularly critical spot in north-eastern Tibet, when the lamas became uneasy about the onward sweep of the Chinese Reds. We talked back and forth with Bob after he had made a report to Reggie on border developments. Bob lives in a remote town where there are naturally no other Europeans. His fellow towns-men speak no English, but he is beginning to pick up some Tibetan. If Ford keeps a diary of his experiences, he undoubtedly will have a great story to tell one of these days.

Reggie spends a considerable part of his time talking to amateur short-wave operators all over the world. He particularly likes to chat with American "hams." And they all seem to want to contact him simultaneously at AC4YN—Lhasa. The instant Reggie goes on the air, scores of amateur radio operators try to lure him into talking with them. Night after night we sat with Reggie while he was carrying on these informal global chats. He has come to regard many of the American short-wave operators as his personal friends, even though he has never seen any of them.

Why does a man like Fox want to stay in Tibet permanently?

"You might say," the stocky, sandy-haired radio man explains, "I like sitting on top of the world. I like this country and its people. Tibet has been good to me, so I see no reason for leaving it."

This is all the more surprising because Fox has a serious health problem. For several years he has been afflicted with arthritic gout, that painful and distressing malady which causes inflammation and swelling of the joints. When we were in Lhasa his feet were so swollen and sore that he stumbled along, tortured, with a cane in each hand. Almost anyone else in that condition would have long since left for the West and medical attention. But not Reggie!

Fox subscribes to an American news weekly. In one issue he read of a new drug that was said to offer complete relief in certain forms of arthritis. He was convinced that his case came in this category. Fox asked what we had heard about this discovery, Cortisone. Although we knew nothing about it, we promised Reggie that we would make a thorough investigation of the new drug when we reached home and, if possible, send him some.

Upon our return to America in late October Dad and I at once inquired about Cortisone. What we learned at first was discouraging—Cortisone, we were told, was only in the experimental stage; furthermore, its manufacture was so difficult that it was impossible to tell when it might be available.

In midwinter Reggie wrote me a long letter telling of a fresh attack of arthritis, the most severe he had ever had, putting him to bed for several weeks. He asked when we could get that wonder drug to him. We could only reply that we were still trying to find a way. A few months later Reggie radioed this message to India, which was relayed to us: "Gouty arthritis now very severe. Please ship medicine soonest."

It was obvious that our British friend had almost reached the limit of his endurance, but what could we do? In desperation we turned for help to the chemical firm that produces Cortisone synthetically, Merck and Company. They listened with interest to our story about Fox. Could anything be done, we asked? They said, "Perhaps." Dr. James Carlisle, Merck medical director, explained that a great deal had been learned about the drug during the winter, and an easier way had been found to produce it. Chances are, he told us, that it could solve Reggie's problem quickly.

Without delay or hesitation the Merck Laboratory turned over to us for shipment to Fox a whole year's supply of this scarce new medicine, worth thousands of dollars, at no cost. As I write these lines, Reggie Fox, the indispensable hub of Tibetan communications, is painfully riding through the Himalayas on his way to Calcutta, where he will receive from United States Consul General Charles Derry the supply of Cortisone which we dispatched by air. We hope it will cure Reggie. If so, it may help to save Tibet.

Although our efforts in Washington to win American aid for the Dalai Lama's country seem to have been in vain, we have had a great deal of satisfaction in being able to relieve Reggie's suffering. At least Dad and I could do that much for Tibet, thanks to the generosity of Merck and Company.

18

ESCAPE TO SHANGRI-LA

THE story of the other two Europeans in Tibet is even more colourful than that of Reggie Fox, who is more at home in Lhasa than in his native London. It concerns two escaped prisoners of war who now live in Lhasa. The story of how they got there may rate as one of the top adventure yarns of our time.

In the spring of 1939 two Austrian mountaineers arrived in the Vale of Kashmir. They had journeyed to India in order to climb Nanga Parbat, one of the unconquered giants of the Himalayas. When they descended from the mountain, Hitler was on the march. Europe was aflame, and they soon found themselves en route to a British POW camp in India. Eventually they escaped from a prison at Dehra Dun, at the foot of the Himalayas, 120 miles north of Delhi. For months they played hide-and-seek with guards along the frontier and with Tibetan officials. They journeyed over lofty mountains, unmapped deserts and ice fields, and eventually made their way into the Forbidden City and were welcomed there.

Years have gone by since the end of World War II, and they are still living on the Roof of the World. Today they are both Tibetan officials, employed by the Dalai Lama. They told us they have decided never to leave the Shangri-La to which they had fled.

The names of these two mountaineers? One, Peter Aufschnaiter, by profession an engineer, is from the picturesque Austrian town of Kitzbuhel. The other is

ESCAPE TO SHANGRI-LA

Henry Harrer of Graz. Peter, the older of the two, is fifty. Henry, a handsome blonde chap, is thirty-six. Prior to the war he was a member of the Austrian Olympic ski team.

As we sat on the roof of the villa in Lhasa where Dad and I were staying, with maps spread out before us, they detailed their story for the first time.

The British had interned them, with other Germans and Austrians, at the Dehra Dun camp. From behind the wire fences they could look out at the row of snow-capped Himalayan peaks, not many miles away. If they could escape to those heights, they knew that few policemen or soldiers in India could follow them.

There were several attempts at freedom, and Harrer and Aufschnaiter were involved in them all. When they finally made it, in April, 1944, they believe it was because a new British officer was in command of the camp, a chap who was not too alert. Parties of workmen often came into the prison compound, natives accompanied by British commissioned or non-commissioned officers. In some way the prisoners had succeeded in accumulating enough British and Indian clothing to disguise themselves. One day, five of them painted their hands and faces with potassium permanganate and posed as Indian workmen. Two others masqueraded as British officers. Then all seven boldly walked out of the prison camp, supposedly part of a work detail.

Henry Harrer was not a member of that escape party. He got out another way. Around the camp were two high wire fences. Between them was a wide space the prisoners called the "chicken run." Over it, at one point, was a roof that extended from one wire fence to the other to provide shelter for the sentry. Henry managed to get across both fences by way of that shelter on the same day as the mass escape took place. He was shot at but missed, and succeeded in reaching the rendezvous at which the fugitives had agreed to meet.

Two of the eight escaped prisoners, donning the stolen British officers' uniforms, headed for a railroad station in an attempt to make their way out of India. The other six struck off for the Himalayas, with Tibet as their goal. At eleven thousand feet, they reached the uninhabited village of Nelang. The villagers, who abandon Nelang every winter when snow clogs the passes, had not yet returned, so the prisoners felt safe. They rested there ten days and made plans to continue on to the Tibetan frontier, still two days distant.

At Nelang, one of the escaped party decided that life behind the wire fences at Dehra Dun was preferable to the icy fastness of the world's bleakest land. He turned back. The remaining five pressed on over the Himalayas, heading for the valley of the Sutlej, one of Central Asia's great rivers.

Here there was a disagreement about which way they should go. The group split up, two men heading west toward the Spiti Valley, a region of Tibet known for its murderous brigands. Peter Aufschnaiter, Henry Harrer and a third man, Kopp, pushed north, with the Indus River Valley as their goal.

Their first objective beyond the frontier was the largest monastery in western Tibet, at Tholing. This abbey is known far and wide in that part of Asia. It is one of the oldest and richest of the lamaseries.

Tibetan officials in Tholing got wind of the three Europeans who were heading that way. Instead of waiting for them to arrive, the Dalai Lama's representative in that far corner of Tibet came out and met them when they were still two days from Tholing. They told the fleeing Austrians they must turn back. At first the Tibetan officials were courteous, almost gentle with them. But when the Tibetans found the three Europeans persistent, they blocked the road and adamantly insisted that the intruders retrace their steps. Nevertheless, the escaping prisoners pushed past them and continued toward Tholing.

Arriving at the great monastery, they asked to see the head abbot. That high lama executive explained that, much as he might like to help them, there was nothing he could do. But he did suggest that they continue for a few days more, and he sent along an escort to take them to the town of Shangtse, a two-days' march to the north-west.

There they were turned over to the top local Tibetan official, the Dzong-pön, governor of the region. The Dzong-pön presented them with ceremonial white silk scarves, ordered a banquet set before them, and gave them endless cups of yak-butter tea. He listened courteously and sympathetically to their story. But he explained that, without orders from Lhasa, there was nothing he could do either. They must go back to India. In fact, he ordered them to go by the most direct route, over Shipki Pass.

With sinking hearts they headed south. But when they came to the border, their hopes rose again. They saw no frontier guards, only a signpost reading: "SIMLA, 200 MILES." Simla, the summer capital of India, was the last place to which they wanted to go.

Luckily, the Dzong-pön of Shangtse had not sent an armed guard to make sure they crossed into India. He had simply ordered them to go. At the Tibet-India border, the escaped prisoners told officials that they were Americans. Even in that far corner of Central Asia there is, or was, magic in the word "American." Aufschnaiter and Harrer had no intention of returning to India. They were determined to stay in Tibet. But their companion, Kopp, left them and went back to Dehra Dun to give himself up.

Without telling the Tibetans on the frontier what they had in mind, the two men detoured into the mountains and then started north-east over a pass seldom traversed even by tribesmen. Its name is Budbud-La, its altitude eighteen thousand feet.

Peter and Henry journeyed by night, keeping away from villages and the tents of nomads. Five days later they descended into the Indus Valley, where they came to one of the great caravan routes of Tibet, the main trade way between Ladakh and Lhasa. It runs east and west from Kashmir to the Dalai Lama's capital. Traders and others who encountered them on this road paid no attention to them.

After five days more of travel along this caravan route they arrived at Gartok, the present-day capital of western Tibet. Here they could not avoid the monk official and the lay noble representing the Dalai Lama. This time luck seemed to be with them. They made friends with the two officials, who allowed them to continue on to the south-east.

But there was a catch in it. They were given this permission only with the understanding that they were to journey along the caravan route for approximately one month. At the end of that time, when they came to a junction where an important trail turns south over the mountains to Nepal, they were to take that route and leave Tibet. The friends they had made at Gartok treated them handsomely, outfitted them with Tibetan clothes, supplied them with food for the journey and gave them three yaks for pack animals.

Eight days south-east of Gartok brought the Austrian pair to one of the fabulous lakes of high Asia. The people of India call it Lake Manasarowar. Sven Hedin, the eminent Swedish explorer, once described it as the most beautiful lake in Asia. The azure lake is regarded as holy by most of the peoples of Central Asia and also by the Hindus. Thousands of pilgrims visit it each year. It is at an altitude of sixteen thousand feet, and is surrounded by snow-capped peaks. One of these, Gurla Mandhata, is twenty-five thousand feet high.

Although Gurla Mandhata is the loftiest mountain over-looking Lake Manasarowar, another alongside it is much more sacred. Mount Kailas, a twenty-two-thousand-foot Himalayan monarch, ranks with the Mount of Olives and with Fujiyama as one of the most revered mountains on earth. To some hundreds of millions of Hindus and Buddhists, Mount Kailas—Paradise of the God Shiva, one of the Hindu Triad, and the deity of cosmic energy—is the most sacred peak in Asia. The Austrians spent several days exploring the surrounding region and then moved on. Day after day, week after week, the two men continued their long trek down the ancient caravan route.

Dame Fortune was still smiling on Aufschnaiter and Harrer. When they approached the intersection of the caravan routes, the place where they had been ordered to turn south into Nepal, they met two high officials with whom they struck up a friendship. Instead of confirming the order given at Gartok, the Tibetans permitted them to stop and rest for a week or two at the small town of Tradun. The officials also gave them a pass to another town that turned out to be by far the most pleasant they encountered in their long and strenuous wanderings. It was the Tibetan village of Kyirong Dzong, at an elevation that Tibetans consider almost sea level—nine thousand feet. The town is below the timber line and, of course, has an entirely different climate from most of the country. The Austrians rested for several months in a glorious spot surrounded by lofty mountains, in the midst of what they described as a wonderful forest.

In the autumn of 1945, they took to the trail again. This time the Tibetan authorities ordered them to journey south into Nepal. Peter and Henry started in that direction; but as soon as darkness descended, they left the caravan route, circled back and headed north, still determined to reach Lhasa. For a week or so they travelled only by night. Then for thirty-four days they journeyed across the Chang Tang, the great northern plain that is the wildest part of Tibet. Making their way over some of the highest passes in

Tibet they drove their pack animals through an almost un-inhabited territory, a land of many rivers and thousands of lakes. All of the rivers in the Chang Tang flow into lakes that have no outlets. These lakes, by the way, are one of Asia's main sources of salt and borax.

During this part of their long jaunt they were in a desolate region where there are no villages. No grain will grow on the lofty plains of the Chang Tang. The only inhabitants are a few nomads and their yaks. It was on this stretch, a few days before Christmas, 1945, that they had their narrowest escape. Peter and Henry noticed that they were being followed. And they were experienced enough to know that the men who were coming up one of the passes behind them were brigands. This is a section of Tibet where it is common knowledge that robbers will murder you merely to steal your clothes. The two Austrian mountaineers eluded the brigands by leaving the narrow footpath and doubling back around one of the peaks. Then they struck out cross-country, travelling over a region of glaciers and rocky cliffs. In January, when they figured they were within a week's journey of Lhasa, they crossed another ice field and arrived at the top of Guring-La, a 19,300-foot snow-swept pass.

Descending from there into the valley of the Kyi Chu, they entered the Forbidden City by night in mid-January, 1946. Their faces were so sunburned and weatherbeaten that they might have passed for almost anything except Europeans. They wore long beards, torn sheepskin outer jackets, and fur hats, and had yak-hair shoes on their weary feet.

Once more, and at the most important time of all, luck was with them. They encountered a Tibetan who was a hospitable, friendly person—Thangmay by name. He invited them to his home. After he heard their story, he passed it along to some of his influential friends.

We suspect the Tibetans had great admiration for these

Austrians—especially for the way they had crossed that 19,300-foot pass in midwinter. At any rate, as the days and weeks went by, they made more and more friends. The officials of the Dalai Lama's government decided that it might be wise to allow them to stay. The two Austrians did everything they could to make themselves valuable. In Tibet there are no engineers, and both men had knowledge that could be put to good use. Slowly they worked their way into the confidence of the Dalai Lama and the men around him.

Months passed, and then years. They virtually became Tibetans. When we were in Lhasa, both men were engaged on important projects. On the outskirts of Lhasa, Peter Aufschnaiter was directing the digging of a canal. Henry Harrer works with the Tibetan Foreign Bureau, and we found him busy revising much-needed maps.

The two wear purple robes, eat Tibetan food and speak the language like natives. The Tibetans are fond of them. They in turn like the Tibetans. So it seems to be an exceedingly satisfactory combination—so much so that both Peter and Henry plan to remain residents of Tibet for the rest of their lives.

When we left Lhasa, Peter and Henry were on hand to bid us goodbye. We asked them whether they would not like to join us and return to their homeland and families.

Peter Aufschnaiter shook his head. "When you look at the aftermath of the war in Europe, do you wonder why Henry and I choose to remain here—with our good and faithful friends in Tibet?"

[In a letter dated May, 1950, Henry writes of his latest Tibetan project: "During the winter I built a small cinema (16 mm. run by a generator) for the Dalai Lama inside the yellow wall at Norbu Linga, and since the day he moved there from the Potala (for his summer residence), we often have shows for him. I have to explain everything and he is so inquisitive and intelligent that it is really amazing. Most of the time we are alone and discuss all sorts of things. Judging from the knowledge and will he shows at sixteen years, he promises to become a great statesman."

What an enviable position Henry is in, so close to the Dalai Lama!]

19

DANGEROUS TRAIL HOME

But all too soon it came time for us to leave Lhasa. Our days passed swiftly, and again the business of organizing a caravan was our most pressing problem. Because the Tibetans are superstitious, we had to leave on a lucky day—Monday, Wednesday or Sunday. If a Tibetan is forced to start a journey on a day that is not auspicious, he often sends his hat or some other article of clothing along the trail by messenger on the lucky day in order to beguile the gods into believing that was when he departed.

Although we left Lhasa on a day of good omen, we failed to dodge the jinx which seems to haunt nearly every caravan of foreigners venturing into the mystical realm of the Dalai Lama. Our misfortune, as is usually the way, came when least expected. We should have been better prepared for it.

We got off from Lhasa with a flying start. A swift ride down the swollen Kyi Chu in skin coracles took us the forty miles to Chusul in six hours—in contrast to the two and a half days we had spent coming in. We continued over the mountains at a fairly rapid pace, hopeful of landing in New York by the first of October. After scaling 16,600-foot Karo-La, we left the glaciers of that lofty pass and led our animals down the steep descent to the Ralung plain.

We were on our fifth day homeward bound from the Holy City, and two days from Gyantse, when the gods frowned.

I was in the lead when Dad, a few yards behind, decided to remount. Suddenly there was a commotion and a scuffle. I turned around in time to see him sail through the air and land on a pile of sharp rocks. His horse had whirled and bolted, throwing him violently to the ground, while he had one foot in the stirrup and the other halfway over the saddle.

Dad was unable to get up—completely out of breath, and white as the mountain snows above us. He struggled to keep consciousness. Such a mishap at an altitude where there's a lean mixture of oxygen can spell the end quickly. A weaker heart might not have withstood the shock. Not until he reached the hospital in New York more than a month later did we learn that he had broken his right leg in eight places, just below the hip.

This turn of fate caught us pretty much off guard. We had no doctor, and our first-aid kit was some miles behind with our slow-moving caravan. It was getting late—only another hour till dark—and it was cold. Ralung, the closest village and our immediate destination, lay more than four miles across the plain. What to do? The nearest medical help, we believed, was in Gyantse, more than two stages away, but even that was doubtful. We could do nothing but wait on the trail, hoping our caravan would catch up with us before dark and that interpreter Tsewong, whom I sent galloping on to Ralung, could round up some villagers to come out to help carry Dad in.

Fortunately, we didn't have to wait too long for our sirdar and his yaks and donkeys. Unloading our bedding, we wrapped Dad in a sleeping bag and lifted him on to an army cot. But our first-aid kit contained no morphine. I had nothing to relieve his agony, to ease the effects of shock.

Four hours later, after a painful ride through the darkness and the cold that goes with the nights at those altitudes, my father at last reached shelter. It was only with the utmost difficulty that the six peasants who had helped me carry him across the plain were able to hoist his folding bed up the rickety ladder that led to the sleeping quarters of the house in which we stayed.

That first night was one of the worst Dad has ever experienced. The shock and exposure brought on high fever and frequent fainting. His shattered hip gave him the very devil. No position was comfortable. Sleep was impossible. It was a long gasping night of agony and worry in just about the most out-of-the-way spot you can find on this planet. Imagine being stricken in a land where the people don't believe in doctors, relying on the lamas to cure their ills through herbs, incantations and ceremony.

Next morning, Tsewong and I hiked to the Ralung telephone. A phone there was a lucky break, for only a few villages along the high road from Gangtok to Lhasa are connected with the one strand of wire that links the two places. I prayed that the line was not down, as it frequently is for weeks on end, and that the Indian army doctor at Gyantse could come to the rescue. It was almost a matter of life or death. Without a doctor to splint Dad's leg, I could see no way ever to get him home.

The phone lineman managed to rouse Gyantse after much shouting and blowing into the ancient battery-driven outfit. Though Gyantse was only thirty-three miles away, the connection was so poor that everything had to be repeated three and four times before it was understood. Nevertheless, we finally reached Rai Bahadur Brahendra Chandra Pal, the Indian army doctor. Tsewong, talking to his brother, a clerk at the Indian trade agency at Gyantse, made our plight known, and Captain Pal agreed to come if permission were granted by the Tibetan Government. Like all his Indian colleagues, the doctor was allowed to go only seven miles beyond Gyantse, the terminus of the Indian mail system. Special authority was necessary to proceed farther into Tibet.

Happily, the Tibetan trade agency gave the nod and the good doctor, one of four in Tibet, made a forced march from Gyantse to reach Ralung in one day. Never was there a more welcome sight to my dad and me than the appearance of the young uniformed Indian—cheerful and smiling in spite of his strenuous all-day ride—when he climbed up the ladder and greeted us at nine that night.

Without an X-ray machine (there is none in Tibet), Dr. Pal could not tell definitely whether Dad's hip was fractured. He explained that medicine, not surgery, was his field; also, that he had had no chance to complete his medical training before he was drafted into the Indian army. As a matter of fact, only one of the four doctors in Tibet is a medical school graduate.

However, after preliminary examination, Dr. Pal said that the injury might be only muscular—torn ligaments and a severe sprain. This was reassuring, and we decided to press on to Gyantse as best we could.

The British explorer Edward Amundsen once said: "The whole of Tibet is like a sea, the gigantic waves of which, driven up by northern and southern winds, have been changed to stone at the moment of their worst fury." That's the terrain we faced for three days, and will remember to the end of our lives.

It sometimes took ten Tibetans to carry Dad's stretcher over the steep rocky trails, which skirted chasms and swift streams, moving at a snail's pace to keep him from plunging into the river far below. Strapped to the stretcher, with his leg in a splint, Dad roasted when the sun was out and nearly froze when it ducked behind the clouds and the cold winds blew up. The first night, at Gobshi, we had to borrow Tibetan tents, sleeping out in the cold. A detachment of soldiers had arrived just ahead of us and taken over all available space in the village. In Tibet no one dares raise a finger to the soldiers, who are accustomed to make up their deficit in salary by helping themselves to anything they fancy.

The next night we were more fortunate, with real beds—*charpis*—at the home of Jigme Tering, a Tibetan country gentleman whom we had met in Lhasa. He had invited us to make his house on the Gyantse road a stopping place on the way home. On the third day we reached Gyantse, and the Mahratta garrison, where the quarters seemed like paradise after those grim days on the trail.

Dr. Pal and Captain Ramchandra Patil, the commanding officer of the Mahratta detachment, were exceedingly cordial. During our ten days with them, their hospitality was unbounded. Dr. Pal watched over Dad as he lay on one of their few Indian-style beds. Incredible though it now seems, after about a week on his back, Dad managed to walk on that badly fractured leg. Assisted only by a cane, he slowly and painfully could stagger from his room to the mess hall some twenty yards away. I think it was sheer will-power and guts that enabled him to walk on that limb, with the femur cracked in eight places. However, at the time, this effort fooled us into concluding that the leg was not broken, and we made plans to continue on to civilization.

An early return was mandatory, too. Soon deep snows would clog the Himalayan passes and we might have been marooned until the summer of 1950. How about having a plane come in to fly us out? This was impossible. The best we could do was to fashion our own magic carpet for Dad—a stout wooden sedan chair, to be carried on the shoulders of Tibetans.

Two weeks after Dad's losing argument with the horse, we hit the trail for home again. And it was a long trail, too. It took us sixteen days to cover the two hundred or more miles from Gyantse to Gangtok, averaging one to two miles per hour. Fortunately, we did have a medical man with us most of the way. Dr. Rai Bahadur Bo, a middle-aged gentleman, was not a graduate doctor but he had studied and practised medicine quite a bit; he accompanied us the first day out of Gyantse to check on Dad's condition after ten hours of bouncing along the trail. The next day Dr. Pal caught up with us on his way to the Indian troops stationed at Yatung. He stayed with us to within one day's march of Yatung, and relieved our anxiety with nightly medical check-ups.

The Tibetans, in teams of four, carried Dad's sedan chair. As they plodded along they chanted or sang to keep in step. Sometimes it was *"Om Mani Padme Hum!"* the familiar prayer to Buddha, which they chanted over and over again. More often, though, they sang a ditty that may be translated as, "O Lord Buddha, lighten our load!" Another thing he could not escape was the continual bounce, bounce, bounce of his wooden litter. Luckily, we had an air mattress with us which we inflated and placed in his chair. But still this did little toward lessening the pain during that bumpy hair-raising journey. At times, Dad had to leave the chair and hobble around sharp turns in the trail that were too abrupt for the coolies to manage with their burden. In some places the path was so narrow that they had to tip the chair on edge to make their way along a canyon wall.

Dad managed to keep his sense of humour, though, and tried to teach the Tibetans new songs. At other times he chanted with them. And at night, in his fitful sleep, he kept on chanting, "O Lord Buddha, lighten our load." (This prayer was answered too, for on that journey Dad lost twenty pounds.)

At Yatung, on the fifth of October, we were met by a rescue team sent out by Loy Henderson, United States Ambassador at New Delhi, with the co-operation of the Indian Government. It consisted of Royal Bisbee, a member of our embassy staff; Emily Bateman, a health officer from the embassy, and Major A. K. Bose, one of

India's leading combat surgeons. Naturally, we were overjoyed to see them, even though we had just about done our own rescuing, and at Yatung we were only a few days from Gangtok. It is impossible to find words to express our gratitude to Ambassador Henderson, the Indian Government and all the others who came to Dad's assistance.

As if the rescue team was not enough, the United States Air Force ordered a plane to the nearest airfield to help with our evacuation if necessary. At Siliguri, just south of Gangtok, the American air attaché to India picked us up in his C-47 and flew us on to Calcutta. From there to America it was no problem. We flew halfway around the globe in the same amount of time it takes to hike forty tortuous miles in the Land of the Lamas.

Once home, no time was lost getting Dad to a hospital, where his leg was operated on successfully. His right femur, which had begun to knit improperly during the month since the accident, was rebroken and properly set. All through the winter and until May Dad was on crutches. But in August, less than a year after that fall, he was able to ski in Alaska on the Juneau Ice Cap.

Our fabulous trip to Lhasa came to an end officially when, on behalf of both of us, I delivered a scroll to President Truman. Receiving me in his office at the White House, the President asked about our journey. So I spread a map before him and pointed out the route we had taken. Mr. Truman studied it for a moment, sighed wistfully and said that he had long dreamed of visiting Lhasa, but that he probably would never have the opportunity.

The message I turned over to President Truman had been handwritten in Tibetan characters with a bamboo pen on parchment made from the bark of a Tibetan tree. It was dated "the sixteenth day of the seventh month of the Earth Bull year (September 7, 1949)," and read:

"Now that Lowell Thomas, Sr., and Lowell Thomas, Jr., have been able to visit Tibet they are well acquainted with all facts about this country. Therefore, the government of Tibet hopes that from them the President of the United States, the people of America, and those who live in other countries as well, will soon come to know more about Tibet. That it is a holy, independent country, a religious country, ruled over by His Holiness, the Dalai Lama, who is the true Incarnation of Chenrezi, the Buddha of Mercy. Furthermore, that all Tibetans, including the civilian population as well as the monks, are entirely devoted to religion.

"We have learned that unfortunately, throughout this world at the present time, there is an absence of peace and happiness—this because of troubles between peoples, and disturbances and conflicts of many kinds. We, the government and people of Tibet, are much worried, deeply concerned over the present state of the world in which we all live. And we are eager to have it known that here in Tibet, a land that is especially dedicated to religion, all of our peoples, both lay and monk, are earnestly praying that God will grant happiness and everlasting peace to all humanity."

APPENDIX

WHEN YOU GO TO TIBET

Anyone who contemplates a journey into Tibet may find the following list of equipment useful. It includes the gear I should like to have in the event of a return trip to Lhasa:

CAMP EQUIPMENT

SLEEPING BAGS. These are preferable to the American Express type bed-rolls, and I recommend using the outer half of the surplus army mountain troop sleeping bag; the inner mummy bag can be dispensed with for temperatures not less than plus 20 degrees Fahrenheit. The outer portion is warm enough for even the coldest nights experienced during the summer and early fall in Tibet at altitudes not greater than fifteen thousand feet. If blankets and sheets are used, each person must have a minimum of four *heavy* woollen blankets and preferably five— in addition to a pillow, three sheets and two pillowcases.

FOLDING COTS. These are essential whenever the party gets away from the dak bungalows that are at regular intervals between Gangtok and Gyantse. Your own cots are needed all the rest of the way. And your own bedding is necessary at all times.

COT PADS. They are necessary, and the heavier the better. Cot pads help greatly against cold draughts that have a way of attacking the cot sleeper from below.

AIR MATTRESSES. Would be a good investment, as they give added protection against cold draughts as well as added comfort. (One extra air mattress, just in case some member of the party has a puncture.)

TENT. We managed to get along without one; still, I would recommend carrying a light tent to use occasionally when the assigned Tibetan peasant's home seems unusually dirty, or when the Dalai Lama's soldiers have arrived ahead of you and commandeered all available space.

GAS LANTERNS. These are absolutely essential—one for the dinner table and to read by, and a second to be used by the cook instead of candles or butter lamps. This makes the servants happier and speeds up the whole kitchen activity. From our experience, where our lanterns were carefully packed for each day's march, I would suggest that two spare mantles per lantern per week be carried; this will be more than enough, as we found that one mantle would often last two weeks.

PRIMUS STOVE. The kind that operates on kerosene is a good investment. While a good cook can work wonders over a dung fire, he can't keep its unpleasant odour from getting into the food. It is nice now and then to have your meal taste almost the way it should; and a Primus stove will speed up the cook's work.

JEEP GAS CANS. Two for carrying kerosene.

PORTABLE CHAIRS, TABLE AND CANVAS BATH. None of these is needed.

RADIO. On a long trip a portable short-wave receiver operated by batteries would be most welcome; one gets a craving for the news after a few weeks in the wilderness.

FLASHLIGHTS. Must be carried; one per person is a reasonable number, with sufficient spare batteries and bulbs. And there should be some for the servants—especially for the sirdar, who will more than once be caught on the trail with the pack train after dark.

SADDLES, BRIDLES AND SADDLE BAGS. We used English flat saddles purchased in Calcutta. While they served the purpose, we feel that American western-type saddles would be more comfortable for all-day riding. In any case, the saddles must be provided with front and tail pieces to keep them in place; and the girths should be sufficiently adjustable so that they can be made to fit snugly around small, scrawny Tibetan ponies. Bridles usually are available at the point where the expedition actually gets under way; for instance, at Gangtok. But they are pretty flimsy. It would be much better to buy, along with the saddles, strong, good-looking bridles. Saddle bags are useful for carrying cameras, canteen, etc. And stout leather riding crops should be carried too. Of course, they must be watched carefully at night—the same goes for most everything else—lest they be stolen. Straps and buckles are highly prized.

THERMOS. Each member of the party needs a canteen for drinking water; also, several small Thermoses (unbreakable if possible) should be included for the purpose of having hot tea or soup on the trail at midday.

FOR THE CARAVAN

BOXES. Very strong wooden boxes of dimensions (in feet) three by one and a half by one are best suited for carrying purposes, and they must be provided with padlocks. A box that is any larger—especially in thickness—is difficult to pack on a donkey and sticks out so far that it is apt to smash against rocks along the trail. (In our case the boxes made for us in Calcutta were too large and had to be cut down in Gangtok.) Also each box or case, when packed, should weigh about fifty pounds, not eighty; a donkey seems to be well loaded with two 50-pound boxes plus the odds and ends that are bound to be placed on the top of his pack saddle. We found that small metal foot-lockers are good for carrying clothing, books, etc. They can stand pretty rough treatment; of course the lighter they are in weight the better. Duralumin would be ideal.

WATERPROOFS. These must be included in sufficient number. One canvas tarp that is about eight by five is big enough to protect one donkey's load.

WATERPROOF CASES. If they are obtainable, they should be used to carry film, gifts and other damageable items up through the monsoon rains of Sikkim.

OUT OF THIS WORLD

STRAPS AND BUCKLES. It would be wise to have a few of each for repair work.

TWINE (STRING). The caravan should carry two balls of stout twine. Some of nylon if you can get it.

TOILET PAPER. Take more than enough.

FOOD

The following is on a basis of two people for one week:

Klim (powdered milk)—three small cans

Sugar—two pounds

Salt—a quarter-pound or less

Pepper—up to the individuals

Butter—one pound (tin)

Paper napkins

Dried fruits—apple rings, apricots, prunes

Canned fruits—whatever is available for variety

Cereals—oatmeal, Cream of Wheat, Maltex, Ralston (variety is the main concern); some dried cereals, in tins, would be a wonderful treat now and then

Bacon—three pounds (tin)

Bread—tinned if possible, plus fresh bread available in Gangtok

Coffee—one 4-ounce tin of Nescafé

Tea—a half-pound (tin)

Cocoa—one tin for two weeks

Ovaltine—one tin for two weeks

Pancake flour—small amount

Maple syrup—small amount just for an occasional treat

Jams—one pound (jar)

Honey—small quantity

Biscuits—(tin)

Cream crackers, water biscuits, and any other variety: one 2-pound tin will last a week

APPENDIX

Cheese—light Swiss, preferably in tins and divided into individual blocks

Sardines—one small can will serve two for one trail lunch

Chocolate—as desired

Raisins, dates, figs—two 1-pound packages

Soups—in tablet form

Canned meat—main thing is quality and variety; roast beef, ham, chicken, hash, lamb stew, ragout de veau, duck

Fish—several kinds

Pork and beans

Vegetables—canned—a good variety

Dried vegetables—if available

Desserts—variety is important again; Jello, canned fruit, tinned puddings.

ADDED ATTRACTIONS

Some bottled sherry and wine

Good Scotch whisky and a few bottles of the best Jamaica rum. Tibetan nobles like both!

Cigars and lots of cigarettes (preferably some American brand never seen before)

Chewing gum

Kleenex—a large supply

One case of books and magazines to read and then either leave in a dak bungalow or give away.

NOTE: On this matter of food I can't over-emphasize the importance of variety. During the first few weeks it is not so vital, but by the second month the same diet day after day gets pretty grim. During the summer in Tibet you can count on being able to procure good fresh mutton, yak meat and eggs. However, no fruit is available, and only a few vegetables; these invariably are cabbage, potatoes, and giant tasteless radish. Rice also can be obtained in towns like Gangtok, Yatung, Phari, Gyantse and Lhasa.

Kerosene is available both at Gyantse and Lhasa (or was in the summer of '49).

Lhasa's bazaar even has shaving soap, pots and pans, small mirrors, flashlights, cigarettes ("battle axes" and English tinned), etc.

KITCHEN EQUIPMENT

Kettles
Frying pan
Nest of pots
Measuring cup
Cooking spoon and fork
Several cook's knives of various sizes
Salt shaker
Drinking cups
Tin plates
Forks, spoons and knives
Plenty of matches and some candles for emergency
Kitchen soap
Dish towels
Steel wool
Wash rags
Can openers

A complete kitchen is needed on the trail—the above list is probably not complete.

CLOTHING

Rain suits of the full-length navy type that are absolutely waterproof, with hoods or separate rain hats

Rubber-soled Barker Boots with extra inner soles; perhaps a pair of ski boots or other warm and rough trail boots

Sun glasses—extras

Old pair of heavy riding breeches for the trail

Good pair of riding breeches for Lhasa (incidentally, as all movement in Lhasa is by mule or by horse, ordinary city pants are not practical—and good-looking riding breeches

are customary for western visitors.) Field-type riding boots
are preferable—easier for walking

Flannel shirts

Light- and medium-weight sweaters

Two pairs long underwear

Cap with ear flaps

Light gloves

Wind-breaker

Sheepskin jacket or other warm coat with fur collar

Slippers—moccasin type, leather or reindeer skin

Broad-brimmed western hat

Plenty of warm socks

Few good linen shirts to wear with warm sports coat and tie
in Lhasa

One pair grey slacks—useful in Lhasa

Two pairs of heavy pyjamas.

MEDICINE KIT

Any expedition to Tibet should go prepared for trouble. The
caravan medicine kit should be as complete as possible, even
including a splint for a broken leg, and morphine. It will be
easy enough to gather together the usual things such as aspirin,
sunburn lotion, etc. Here are a few suggestions that I have
after our trip:

Zinc oxide ointment for sunburnt lips

Sunburn lotion

Bandaids and iodine

Cotton

Gauze

Adhesive tape

Good disinfectant such as alcohol

Vaseline

Whitfield's ointment for athlete's foot or ringworm

Foot powder

Sulpha pills and penicillin with careful instructions from an M.D.

Plenty of tablets for purifying water

Laxatives—we had a great deal of trouble in this respect owing to diet. Mild as well as strong laxatives should be included in the kit—I would suggest Milk of Magnesia, Ex-Lax and mineral oil. This is important. It might be wise to take something mild to be eaten each morning with your breakfast food.

The best advice I can give is to make up a medicine kit with the advice of a doctor. But by all means be sure to include some sedatives, sleeping pills most certainly, and morphine in case of accident. The ideal thing would be to take a doctor along on any trip into such remote country.

NOTE. You must have dak bungalow passes. These from the political officer, Gangtok.

GIFTS

One of the best ways of pleasing the nobles would be to present those who are interested with fine bottles of sherry, or some good wine. Whisky also would make a real hit with people like Tsarong, Shakabpa, etc.

Incidentally, Reggie Fox, who runs the Dalai Lama's 16-mm. projector, said that 16-mm. Tarzan films or Marx Brothers films would make a big hit with the Dalai Lama and those around him. They most certainly don't want to see any pictures where human or animal life is taken; amusement and adventure are the things that they are interested in.

A FEW RANDOM THOUGHTS

By all means take along a big book containing photos of America. Also a folder containing photos of your own home, etc.

APPENDIX

Extra raincoats should be taken for your servants.

And you must take some of your own letter paper and envelopes because you will have to write letters, answering invitations to parties, etc., in Lhasa, and there is no decent stationery in this city.

Money

Indian *paper* rupees.

INDEX OF PERSONS

INDEX OF PERSONS

INDEX OF PLACES

INDEX OF PLACES